PROSPERITY
IN
CHINA

PROSPERITY IN CHINA

International Responsibility
and Opportunity for a
GROWING POWER

JIN CANRONG

New York   Chicago   San Francisco   Athens   London
Madrid   Mexico City   Milan   New Delhi
Singapore   Sydney   Toronto

Beijing Jinghua Hucais Printing, Co., Ltd.

ISBN   978-0-07-181992-3
MHID   0-07-181992-4

e-ISBN   978-0-07-181993-0
e-MHID   0-07-181993-2

Library of Congress Cataloging-in-Publication Data
Canrong, Jin.
  Prosperity in China : international responsibility and opportunity for a growing power / Jin Canrong.
      pages cm
  ISBN-13: 978-0-07-181992-3 (hardback : alk. paper)
  ISBN-10: 0-07-181992-4 (hardback : alk. paper) 1. China—Foreign economic relations. 2. China—Relations. 3. China—Economc conditions—21st century. I. Title.
  HF1604.C257 2014
  337.51—dc23
                                                                              2013030192

McGraw-Hill Education books are available at special quantity discounts to use as premiums and sales promotions or for use in corporate training programs. To contact a representative, please visit the Contact Us pages at www.mhprofessional.com.

CONTENTS

PREFACE

According to the history of modern international relations, a country acquires its leadership along with internal domestic demand and the external needs of its international responsibilities. It is a basic fact in international relations that a country is unlikely to win respect and acknowledgment on its way to the center of the international arena if it fails to positively engage in international affairs and to solve problems in the international community. In terms of geography, population, economy, and resources, China is inherently a great power with a long history and a complicated domestic situation. The country has witnessed the suffering of the Chinese nation as well as the nation's development from poverty and underdevelopment to prosperity.

During the late 1970s and the early 1980s, with the implementation of the reform and opening-up policy, China began to speed up the process of integration into the international system. Due to the arduous efforts of several generations, the country has gradually accumulated its national strength, improved its image, and changed its international conduct. By the beginning of the twenty-first century, China's development was drawing the continuing and widespread concern of the international community. As a focus of different kinds of opinions and views, the old "new star" is once again attracting the attention of the world.

It is an unavoidable reality that China is on its way to the center of the world arena, from an unimportant walk-on role to a supporting role and the best-supporting role, then the leading role and maybe the core leading role in the future. China has kept its rapid growth for over 10 years and become the most powerful engine driving the world economy, while the Western countries have been trapped by the sluggish economy and a world shadowed by financial crisis. When those "Made in China" marks cross the border and flood into the world, when the "China Model" is hailed by more and more of the developing countries, when the "Harmonious China" turns into the new pilgrimage destination of the world diplomacy, and when China's "Dream Factories" become the paradise for global investors. Then the concept of "China's Responsibilities" is definitely the focus of the world.

It is not necessary for a great power to be a hegemonic one, but it must have a direction. So, what is the direction? It is the first time for the world to require China to be responsible on a large scale, which to some extent acknowledges China's contribution to the world. In 2005, Robert Zoellick, then U.S. deputy secretary of state, called on China to be a "responsible stakeholder" in his famous speech "Whither China: From Membership to Responsibility?" After that, the "responsible stakeholder" put forward by the United States becomes a fashionable phrase when other countries talk about China.

Fueled by relevant circles in the United States and followed by the other parts of the world, suddenly the expectations and criticism of "China's Responsibility" become interwoven, and external pressure and attention are focusing on the "great-power responsibility." Topics such as "financial responsibility," "humanitarian responsibility," "climate responsibility," "responsibility of global governance," "responsibility of international security," "responsibility of exchange rate," and so on are raised one after another. Such issues as food security, climate change, energy consumption, and humanitarian crisis are also aimed at China. It seems that the world revolves around China: on one hand, excessive praise about China's importance is appalling; on the other hand, exaggeration of China's responsibility—meant to confuse the public—has overpowered certain perceptions.

It is the result of the objective situation rather than our subjective design that China has been pushed to the center of the world arena. Regardless of our will, it is because of the growth of Chinese power that China is compelled to take on some international responsibilities.

In fact, the Chinese are not afraid of taking on responsibilities because they always have a strong sense of responsibility. As the saying goes, everybody is responsible for the fate of his country. And the Chinese believe that it is what you can do for the world instead of what the world can do for you that matters.

Facing the responsibilities a great power should assume, China neither avoids them cowardly nor overexerts itself rashly, but according to its capability and each situation, it will resolutely take on the international responsibilities matching its own power, status, and position. In theory, China has proposed many advanced concepts reflecting the development trend of the international community and China's responsible attitude and goodwill to maintain the international order, such as "peaceful coexistence," "seeking common ground while reserving differences," "new security concept," "harmony, security, and prosperity for neighbors," "peaceful development," and a "harmonious world." In practice, China has actively taken on international responsibilities involving important world issues of common concern as well as regional hot issues by finding correct and effective ways to solve real problems seriously and maintain the peace and development of the world.

As far as responsibility is concerned, China's development embodies a system of responsibility; that is, its overall development strategy is under the framework of the current international system rather than making a fresh start by breaking that system. If China adopted a different system, the international order would be unstable. Therefore, China has already made contributions to world peace and development by joining in the existing system. Besides, China's development also reflects the responsibility of governance.

In the past 30 years, China has lifted 400 million people out of absolute poverty, which is a miracle in human history. Meanwhile, the fact that China has established a basically well-off society has itself made pioneering contributions to the practices of human society governance, which is the second-largest contribution to the world. From the diplomatic point of view, China has undertaken a number of international responsibilities and fulfilled corresponding obligations in specific areas. As a permanent member of the United Nations Security

Council, China is endeavoring to positively take responsibility for the safeguarding of world peace by actively participating in UN peacekeeping operations and to promote regional peace and stability; it firmly safeguards the international regime of nuclear weapons nonproliferation and promotes nuclear disarmament; it mediates to solve the two nuclear issues involved with the Democratic People's Republic of Korea (DPRK, or North Korea) and Iran by peaceful, fair, and equitable negotiations, dialogue, and consultation by advocating the replacement of confrontation, nonsolution, and military power with communication, reconciliation, and diplomatic power; and it appoints envoys and coordinates with many entities to promote the Middle East peace process, to resolve regional conflicts, and to resolve the humanitarian crisis.

As the biggest developing country in the world, China itself helps developing countries out of poverty and seeks a common development road. In this respect, China coordinates standing point with other developing countries and promotes the interests of developing countries on international multilateral occasions; and it enhances South-South cooperation to achieve mutual complements in economy. For least-developed countries, it reduces tariff and debts, provides aids and loans, and collaborates with them for the well-being of peoples, the improvement of human rights situations, and the elimination of poverty. As an emerging-market country itself together with many non-Western emerging countries, China actively promotes internal reform so as to effect huge economic achievements and take part in international mechanisms and systems. From the G-8 to the G-8 plus 5 and then the G-20, China is gradually changing the international decision-making mechanism and the Western-led international-discourse powers with its significant improvement in international status and influence. As an active constructor of the international system, China participates in international mechanisms by joining in and observing international treaties and reforming and maintaining existing international systems. In response to humankind's common challenges such as climate change, terrorism, epidemics, and environment problems, China stands with the world through thick and thin and searches for solutions—together. Currently, the trend is becoming more and more obvious that China cannot develop itself in isolation from the world, and the world cannot achieve prosperity and stability without China.

A mature power is rational and sticks to its principles instead of following others. It also understands that it can estimate the strength of its opponents only by estimating correctly its own strength and that its own well-being is essential to the well-being of the world. Undoubtedly, China is still not fully experienced in fulfilling its responsibilities and demonstrating the image of a responsible power, and it should further improve its approaches and enhance its overall ability to so fulfill those international responsibilities.

China should establish and adjust a great-power mentality. Mentality decides cognition, and cognition influences action. At present, China's national mentality is in an adaptation period, so it is essential to establish that great-power mentality. What is a great-power mentality? It should be pursued at least in the following aspects. For instance, obtaining a great-power mentality means more optimism and confidence, a stronger sense of responsibility, and a more objective and rational understanding of China and the world, thus demonstrating a broad mind suitable to great-power status. In this way, China should express the unity, reason, wisdom, and courage of its people and the openness, tolerance, self-confidence, and self-reliance of the country but act neither arrogant nor humble. It should try to get rid of the "century-long national humiliation" complex and keep an ordinary mentality the way a great power should do instead of swinging between low self-esteem and overconfidence.

Besides, the great-power mentality means acquiring a sense of crisis, risks, and challenges. The country should be conscious of its own shortcomings and then improve and perfect itself as if it is walking on eggs all the time instead of being arrogant, so that it won't get lost in praise or depressed by criticism. A country with the great-power mentality is mentally mature and has the abilities to withstand risks, storms, and challenges by reminding itself about adversity in prosperity and about chaos in peace. What's more, a country with the great-power mentality should be responsible and sympathetic for the weak, advocate equality and justice, and work for the well-being of the people and the peace of the world. It never bullies the weak because of its strength, never follows others as it complies with the trend, and never overexalts the West when integrating into the world. It should have its independent voice, distinct characteristics, and correct position.

China also should devote more energy to its domestic governance. According to the history of international relations, no great power would have taken on international responsibilities incompatible with its strength before solving its domestic governance problems. In other words, every country must consider the reality that capacity assumes responsibility. And it is a great responsibility for China to get its own things done. Therefore, the internal requirement before China takes on international responsibility is to develop and enhance its own power. China should above all solve its own problems in the process of development; then it will acquire the moral strength for international responsibilities and enjoy the appeal of playing a leading role.

Although China has made great progress in economic development, it has a series of problems, such as an unreasonable economic structure, emerging governance crises, severe poverty, an unsustainable growth pattern, complicated social conflicts, a widening gap between the rich and the poor, and environmental pollution and damages. It is basic and prerequisite that China take international responsibilities *after* it handles its domestic governance problems, coordinates the country and society, and is keeping the country healthy and vital, which follows the philosophic truth that the development of things depends fundamentally on internal causes and won't be changed on impulse by leaders or the masses.

Currently, the aging of China's population is accelerating and economic growth slowing down because of declining demographic dividends, so the domestic governance challenges will become even more serious. In addition, many fields call for efforts and costs, such as curbing environmental pollution and climate change, shutting down heavy-polluting and high-energy-consuming industries, increasing investment and equipment, and encouraging intelligent, smart, and growth-oriented emerging industries. In this process, there will be certain reductions in taxes and GDP and the pressure of unemployment. Facing those strategic predicaments and even some external criticisms, China should focus on development and not confront others. Only by keeping a low profile and focusing on its own development will China become capable of fulfilling its responsibilities when it is ready to. And all of the existing problems can likely be solved when it devotes all of its time and energy to development.

China also must maintain the balance of four main relations. First, it should balance the relation between internal and external affairs. The great power's responsibilities consist of two parts: the international responsibilities and the domestic ones. China will lose both sides if it concentrates on just one. Compared with external affairs, the issues of domestic society, economy, equality, and justice and the issues about people's livelihoods—housing, employment, medical care, and anticorruption—attract more attention from the people. A large number of people still hold the opinions that a poor China is too lavish on assistance abroad in the world and that it is better to help itself rather than others. They cannot understand China's generous behaviors in the international community because they lack rational knowledge of the international affairs demanding China's proactive intervention. Therefore, it is particularly significant to coordinate the subtle relations between internal and external affairs, foster people's international perspective, deepen their understanding of overseas interests, and win wide support, which will provide sustainable energy for China to fulfill its responsibilities and demonstrate the image of a responsible power.

Second, China should balance the relation between developing and developed countries. China pursues its self-orientation as a developing country, represents the interests of developing countries, and has held consistent positions with those countries in major issues. Meanwhile, China also collaborates and shares interests widely with developed countries, especially on improving trade, addressing global issues, and developing the current international mechanism. And

China holds similar basic positions on promoting the settlement of regional conflicts as well as peace and stability in the world. As the bridge connecting the two sides, China—which advocates harmony and diversity—keeps balance between developed and developing countries and improves dialogues between them by affirming its own position without denying the positions of others.

Third, China should balance the relation between foreign economic cooperation and national image building. Economic development is currently the priority among all tasks, and it calls for international market and energy supply. When China's thirst for oil is greatly increasing, the Western world feels threatened by China's search for oil all over the world, which provides an excuse for neocolonialism. In fact, it is China's consistent principle to develop friendly diplomatic relations everywhere, and China's diplomatic tradition insists on paying much more attention to giving instead of gaining. However, the Western media consider that China comes for economic interests, which is a terrible misunderstanding. Actually, on the principle of mutual benefit, China never imposes on others what it dislikes itself, and it never forces others to accept what it likes. Changing the West's misunderstanding requires plenty of cultural exchange, nongovernment contact, publications, diplomatic work, and military presentation as well as participation in international multilateral collaboration and maintenance of the country's good image. China is supposed to establish a new, emerging-power image that is simple and fresh and different from traditional powers through many channels and on many different levels.

Fourth, China should balance the relation between harshness and sensitivity in diplomacy. Diplomacy means peaceful politics. China should pay attention to methods and skills rather than foolhardiness to leave enough leeway, always showing a smiling face to others. With strong public influence on decision making in foreign policies, it is more important to keep balance between making rational decisions and responding to nationalist sentiment—in order to avoid major strategic mistakes. Therefore, China should keep a low profile and a level of sensitivity on the strategic level for giving first rank to domestic problems; on the tactical level, it has to take part in the world actively to protect its expanding national interest and take on corresponding international responsibilities. In short, China will perform international responsibilities better by a *combination* of harshness and sensitivity.

Moreover, China should take on its international responsibilities actively and selectively. As to the progress of the real situation, China is being pushed to the center of the international arena, so it is forced to undertake certain international responsibilities regardless of its willingness to do so. China needs to deal with two main issues to transform from passivity to initiative: The first one is to eliminate the gap of cognition and take responsibilities voluntarily. On one hand, China has to realize the international community's expectation, and it is impossible to ignore it. On the other hand, with its complicated domestic situations, China is unlikely to behave in accordance with the requirements of the international community, which will lead to conflicts. China is not almighty and cannot solve every problem. Because everything has a limit, to take on international responsibilities voluntarily does not mean to take on too much responsibility or to fulfill the great power's obligation or to undertake excessive duties. On the contrary, with too many responsibilities, China would not perform its normal duties perfectly and could not make due contributions. Hence, China has to realize that as a great power of huge economic size, it should be ready to take on international responsibilities actively and selectively because the international community has many specific requirements.

The second issue is to set more agendas proactively and put forward China's own propositions more clearly so as to reduce passivity on the responsibility agenda setting and improve China's ability to control the agenda—for example, on carbon emission trading issues, nuclear problems with Iran and the DPRK, the world economic recovery and balance, and new energy development. China should pay attention to the most essential issues so that it can respond to its unavoidable responsibilities as well as put forward effective solutions to a few major international problems. Therefore, China expresses its attitude and determination to take on international responsibilities actively, and at the same time, it has the methods and abilities to take them on. China should maintain a tradition of friendship, advocate peace talks, deal with crisis, overcome hatred, and promote democratization and harmonization in international relations based on its own capacity, advantages, and reality.

So even though it is true that the West dominates international discourse and leads opinions and views about China's responsibilities, what are the opinions of the Chinese? How can China's voice be heard and its self-interpretation understood in the world? What we try to do is to add some Chinese seasoning to the Western-style steak. Foreign readers who care about China's emergence and its relation with the West will be attracted by that Chinese flavor. It is our goal that the world could get more interested in and could labor under less misunderstanding of China if it had renewed and fresh opinions.

This book intends to provide a platform whereby people will come to understand and recognize China's international responsibilities to maintain world peace and development. It will also serve as a bridge for China's friends in the world to care more about China's own stories, as contacts and communications lead to friendly coexistence and the harmonious development of peoples and countries.

Jin Canrong

ORIGIN OF INTERNATIONAL RESPONSIBILITIES

In the long history of the Middle Ages, Europe was a huge society connected through feudal subordination, church network, and aristocratic kinship. There were many kings but no genuine nation-states; there were various relationships and responsibilities, held between kings and aristocrats, between city-states, between churches and monks, but no international responsibilities as what we find today. Rights and obligations between nations did not become an issue until the Thirty Years' War in the seventeenth century, which resulted in the creation of many nation-states throughout Europe.

Relations between nation-states, however, do not necessarily include international responsibilities. Around 1 CE, the Han Empire of China, the Persian Empire, and the Roman Empire existed simultaneously in Eurasia. Though they established a connection via the Silk Road, obviously no international responsibility existed between these three great empires. This situation lasted for nearly two thousand years. In that long stretch of time, scientific and technological inventions, luxury goods, and secular philosophies of China flowed into Europe, and a stream of European missionaries and merchants came to China. But when King George III of Britain and Emperor Qianlong of the Qing Dynasty wrote to each other in the nineteenth century, they held diametrically different views about each other's responsibilities. King George III took it for granted that China was no different from France, Prussia, and tsarist Russia in Europe and should act as modern European nation-states; and Emperor Qianlong admitted Britain as a member of the Chinese tributary system and commended it in a magnanimous manner.

One conclusion provides an explanation of these differing views by these rulers: China and Britain were not in the same international system until the early nineteenth century. That situation soon changed due to the British colonial invasion of China. Defeat in the war forced the descendants of Emperor Qianlong to give up the god-given position of "central power" and to begin accepting and integrating into the modern nation-state system established according to the European principle.

Evidently, the establishment of an international system does not depend on the number of nations and the history of their association but, rather, on the political rights and obligations commonly acknowledged by the nations. The rights and obligations can be expressly stipulated in international treaties and international laws or simply accommodated through international norms, practices, and values.

The theories of John Locke and Jean-Jacques Rousseau can serve as a good analogy for this situation. If the international system is a special "society" consisting of nations, it also has a "social contract." Nations agree on rights and obligations according to the contracts and thus form the international system. Different international systems can have different geographic scopes, power structures, and development levels, but a set of rights and obligations is necessary. The international system is an aggregation of nations interconnected through international contracts.

Therefore, international responsibilities form a fundamental element in any international system. As long as a nation is part of an international system, it inevitably accepts in part or in whole the relevant contracts of the system, thus fulfilling its obligations and enjoying its rights. International responsibilities are the foreign obligations a nation undertakes in an international system. Based on that concept, a nation's international responsibilities comprise three levels.

Fundamental International Responsibility

The first level is the responsibility to fulfill international contracts. International contracts include the treaties a nation has signed and the international laws, norms, and fundamental common values it abides by. Performance of international contracts is a basic duty of a nation as a member of an international system, as well as a basic prerequisite for staying in a certain system. If a nation does not recognize or fulfill most of its international contracts, it either withdraws from the system or transforms it thoroughly, according to its own aspiration. Except for the terms of expressly stipulated treaties and legal documents, a member of an international community is duty bound to esteem the values upheld commonly in that international community such as economic development, human rights, and sovereign equality. Obviously, the responsibility of fulfilling international contracts is an *equal* responsibility. There is no *varying* degree of responsibility for nations—only a "fundamental international responsibility."

Limited Responsibility

The second level is the responsibility to maintain international contracts. Nations have rights and obligations according to explicit or implicit contracts, thus forming a set of international rules and regulations, the operation of which has costs. Stakeholders must undertake or share the costs, providing international "public products." The United Nations and its affiliated organizations represent the typical example, maintained by the membership's contributions or by loans offered by member states. Another responsibility of defending international rules and regulations is to stop sabotage. In case of events that could endanger the operation of international rules and regulations, relevant nations must discipline the violator or restore the violated order—for example, via the UN's collective security mechanism and international peacekeeping operations.

The levels of desire and ability to maintain international rules and regulations are different among different nations. Generally speaking, the greater a nation's comprehensive national strength, the stronger its ability to maintain the international rules and regulations; the more a nation benefits from the existing international rules and regulations, the stronger its desire to defend them. In a relatively balanced international system, great powers are usually the leaders as well as the main beneficiaries of the rules and regulations. Their desire and ability to safeguard the international rules and regulations are the strongest.

In sum, at the level of maintaining international rules and regulations, different nations shoulder different international responsibilities. Great powers often bear more responsibilities. Therefore we call this level of responsibility the "limited responsibility."

Leadership Responsibility

The third level is the responsibility to reform international rules and regulations. In international politics, it is the great powers that make history. It is such a prevalent phenomenon of great powers' reforming of the international system that Henry Kissinger exclaimed in his masterpiece *Diplomacy*:

> Almost as if according to some natural law, in every century there seems to emerge a country with the power, the will, and the intellectual and moral impetus to shape the entire international system in accordance with its own values.[1]

Kissinger implied that for self-appointed international leaders at present or in the future, reform of the international system is a responsibility. Such a system is never stationary or stagnant. New powers are emerging, technologies progressing, social productivity developing, people's lifestyles changing, and new philosophies and values forming. Leaders of the international community must adjust the international rules and regulations according to those changes and their own desires and needs in order to retain hegemony. The Westphalia System dominated by France in the seventeenth century, the Vienna system based on the Quadruple Alliance in the nineteenth century, and the American hegemony established at the end of two world wars are all successful examples of responses to challenges and reforms of the international order.

Meanwhile, emerging powers hope to reflect new power contrast in the international order. In history, the rift between the new power structure and the old international order is the main source of the quake of international systems.[2] Some revolutionary countries would rather substantially reshape the international order according to new values and interest patterns if it is hopeless to adjust old international order through "reforms." France in the Revolution, Germany and Japan in the early 1900s, and the Soviet Union in the Cold War are all examples of trying to thoroughly "reshape" international rules and regulations.

Both the countries maintaining hegemony through reform of the international order and those fighting for hegemony through a complete reshaping of the international order are able and ready to play leading roles in the international system. Therefore, we call the third international responsibility the "leadership responsibility."

Development of China's International Responsibilities

There is a complicated debate over China's international responsibilities, dating back to the colonial wars in the mid-1800s. Those wars altered the original international order in Asia, causing China to enter into the world's nation-state system based on the European principle. The content of China's first collection of contracts with the new international system included cession of several million square kilometers of territory with a gradual loss of diplomacy, trade, tariff, and judiciary sovereignty. Therefore, over several decades, China's international responsibility was largely to make sacrifice as a colony. The historical memory of that humiliation is deeply etched in the minds of the Chinese people, so that they still harbor dislike of any international intervention.

Meanwhile, China was unable to fulfill the fundamental responsibilities of maintaining its people's living standard, safeguarding basic human rights, and developing economy due largely to the ravages of colonial wars and exploitation of colonial treaties. Endless wars and economic breakdown reduced China to a failed state, its government unable to safeguard people's basic subsistence, with tens of millions of lives lost in wars and famines. The situation lasted until the essential turning point in 1949, when the People's Republic of China was founded.

But it was also in this most difficult period that China gradually established relations with the modern international community. China began to learn and accept the rules, regulations, norms, and values of a modern international system in the process of revolutions and reforms. Chinese people study with zeal the advanced science and technologies as well as the institutions of the West and set the aim of growing into a "modernized country" like Britain, the United States, or Japan. China has strived to integrate into the international system, hoping to become an equal member of the international community, undertaking its due international responsibilities with great efforts.

As early as the establishment of the League of Nations, China was one of the first members. In World War II, China became one of the Allies—with great national sacrifices—and in the postwar years, one of the permanent members of the UN Security Council. Awakened from the dream of the Celestial Empire, China has been adapting itself to the new role at great speed.

After World War II, the collapse of the European colonial system changed the rules and regulations—as well as the values—of the international system and in some ways reshaped the meaning of international responsibilities. At least in the legal sense, many countries' responsibilities of sacrifice as colonies were abolished. Countries in Asia, Africa, and Latin America gained equal basic international rights with developed Western countries, but for the newly independent former colonies, the international order in the Cold War era was still harsh. Although the United States and the Soviet Union, as emerging hegemonies, inherited most of the basic rules of the traditional European international system, they actually formed two significantly different and confrontational blocs by establishing different alliances, different international organizations, and different ideological systems. Other countries would choose specific international responsibilities when they chose to join one of the blocs.

The newly founded People's Republic of China at first chose to join the Soviet bloc and played a role second only to the role of the Soviet Union, undertaking important "limited responsibility" and to some extent "leadership responsibility." The two wars in that period—the

Korean War and the First Indochina War—were symbols of China's international responsibilities as an important power in the socialist bloc. Largely out of a sense of responsibility as a socialist power, China supported the DPRK, which was at war with the United States in the 1950s and which supported the Democratic Republic of Vietnam at war with the colonial authority in Vietnam. China believed it had the responsibility of maintaining the survival, unity, and development of socialist countries in the world, especially in Asia, and it ended up deeply involved in the Cold War.

Beginning in the late 1950s, China and the Soviet Union gradually became hostile toward each other, and the two countries finally disjoined, resulting in major changes in China's international responsibilities. China no longer shouldered the alliance responsibility as a member of the Soviet military bloc, and it reorientated itself as a socialist power in the so-called Third World. China concentrated on expanding its relations with former colonial countries in Asia, Africa, and Latin America. In the Third World, China promoted international norms and values such as anticolonialism and the five principles of peaceful coexistence and provided economic aid for dozens of countries despite its own economic difficulties. China's generous assistance was rewarded: in 1971, thanks to support by Asian, African, and Latin American countries, the People's Republic of China returned to the United Nations. China's close relationship with the Third World had had a great impact on China's diplomatic tradition, creating a lasting legacy.

The reform and opening-up policy starting from the late 1970s brought China's international vision into another new era. Deng Xiaoping made a monumental statement that peace and development are the two major themes of the world. China began to set economic development as a priority among all goals. Under the general guideline of making economic development the center, the Chinese government developed a concept of international responsibility in which it clearly declared that China regarded raising people's living standards as the most fundamental national responsibility. In other words, China's view of international responsibilities since the implementation of the reform and opening-up policy has centered on dynamic economic development.

China's economic reform has achieved a level of success far higher than expected. In 30 years, China's economy witnessed an average annual growth rate of approximately 10 percent, causing China's economy to double rapidly. Most of the development goals of China's economy set by Deng Xiaoping were achieved ahead of time. China's total GDP ranked fifteenth in 1978 and rose to second in 2010, only after that of the United States.[3]

As early as October 1994, soon after the end of the Cold War and in a speech at the People's Liberation Army's National Defense University, then secretary of defense William Perry of the Clinton administration pointed out the importance of the relationship between the United States and China.[4] In a speech in Seattle in October 1995 on the U.S. policy of engagement with China, Perry also pointed out that an engagement strategy was the best choice for China, which would ensure that China became a responsible international member.[5] Both the 1997 U.S. National Security Strategy and the Quadrennial Defense Review issued by the U.S. Department of Defense mentioned the expectation of China's becoming a responsible member of the international community and the significance of that membership. Former assistant secretary of state James Kelly held a realistic but more moderate view of China in testimony submitted to the Senate Foreign Relations Committee in 2001, which said, "We should pay attention to China's reply to us. We encourage China to make the choices which reflect its status and international responsibility."

After taking office, President George W. Bush said he viewed China as a strategic rival and adopted a preventive containment strategy toward China. As a result, the relatively positive concept of "China's responsibilities" was often overwhelmed by the "China threat theory" and other negative arguments. In Bush's second term after 2005, however, the United States adjust its strategic positioning and China policy, making China's responsibilities the mainstream of U.S. "engagement" policy toward China. In 2005, Bush himself proposed engaging China in a constructive and open way. Secretary of State Condoleezza Rice said the United States hoped China would become one of its global partners and would undertake international responsibility matching its ability.

Deputy Secretary of State Robert Zoellick appealed to China to become a responsible "stakeholder" in the international community in his famous speech "Whither China: From Membership to Responsibility?" Afterward, responsible "stakeholder" was written into the 2006 U.S. National Security Strategy and became a new U.S. official positioning toward China. The Princeton Project Report, issued on September 27, 2006, reflecting the mainstream views of the U.S. elites of all circles and possibly influencing profoundly the U.S. national security strategy, asserted that "America's goal should not be to block or contain China but, rather, to help it achieve its legitimate ambitions within the current international order and become a responsible stakeholder." "Responsible stakeholder" driven by the United States became a buzzword expression in discussions about China in the international community. The United States continued to play up the term, and other countries and regions of the world followed. In this situation, "China's responsibilities" overwhelmingly constituted the major international public opinion environment faced by China.

After the international financial crisis of 2008, further discussions about China's role proliferated in Western countries. On September 15, 2009, Lehman Brothers, a 158-year-old American investment bank, collapsed. The subprime problem within the U.S. banking system had evolved into a global financial crisis, yet the impact on China was relatively small. The international community's expectation for China further increased, the epitome of which was the wording of G-2 and Chinamerica. The idea of G-2 was put forward in the July–August issue of *Foreign Affairs* in 2008 by C. Fred Bergsten, director of the Peterson Institute for International Economics in Washington. Bergsten wrote that the United States should seek to develop a genuine partnership with China to achieve common leadership of the global economic system instead of dwelling on issues that may have arisen within the bilateral relationship.

"Recovery Rides on the 'G2'," written by Robert Zoellick and Yifu Lin for the *Washington Post*, pointed out that for the world's economy to recover, the two economic powerhouses of China and the

United States must cooperate and become the engine for the Group of 20. Niall Ferguson, professor at Harvard Business School, went even further, proposing the concept of Chimerica. In his view, China and the United States have entered a "symbiotic era" and should cooperate with each other, the United States being the world's largest consumer and China the largest saver, with the United States responsible for consumption and China responsible for production of goods.

In 2009, British scholar Martin Jacques's book *When China Rules the World* put forward a systematic theory that China would surpass the United States.[6] *Newsweek* issued a feature article on that book, titled "It's China's World. We're Just Living in It."[7] China's role as a pioneer of a new international system has been a surprise to most Chinese people.

Debate over China's Responsibilities and Its Nature

Is China a responsible power? After Zoellick put forward the concept of "stakeholder," that question has become the focus of Western interrogation of China. The Chinese people discover that on issues about Myanmar, Sudan, and Zimbabwe; on the DPRK nuclear issue and the Iranian nuclear issue; on global warming and environmental issues; on issues of the renminbi (RMB) exchange rate and global trade balance; and on military transparency, Western countries always remind China of its "responsibilities."

In the eyes of many Chinese, this interrogation is unfair. From both the historical and practical points of view, China is a power willing to take on responsibilities. China's economic development and poverty alleviation achievements are evidence of China's responsibilities for the international community. Even in difficult times, China has adhered to a large number of foreign aid operations, which are still increasing. China shoulders international responsibilities in accordance with its own capabilities and in conformity with both the Charter of the United Nations and the rules of relevant UN organizations.

China has good records in the observation of international law and international treaties. Many Chinese therefore believe that China's "international responsibilities" are only a pretense of the West.

In summary, China and the West each stick to their own arguments on China's responsibilities. The debate is difficult because it consists of a mix of consensus, disagreements, differing fundamental views, and complex emotions. The three levels of responsibility—"fundamental responsibility," "limited responsibility," and "leadership responsibility"—will help clarify the nature of the debate over China's responsibilities.

At the level of fundamental responsibility, China and the West actually have more consensus than differences. Most of the Western countries admit that since introduction of the reform and opening-up policy, China has been a model for developing countries in elevating its people's living standard and safeguarding their basic rights. China is also a faithful observer of international law, making endless efforts to integrate into and play a role in international organizations. China pursues the values of sovereign equality and peaceful coexistence, building a good reputation among countries in Asia, Africa, and Latin America. Moreover, China claims to accept the universal values of modern society.

At the level of fundamental responsibility, disagreement between China and the West involves human rights, including the autonomy of ethnic groups. The nature of the dispute is whether a country can stretch across a national border for maintaining basic human rights. After the Cold War, Western countries frequently got involved in other countries' national autonomous movements and internal separatist activities. As a former semicolony, China holds that respect for national sovereign interdependence and territorial integrity is the most fundamental contract in the modern international system, the waiving of which would undermine the root of the international system. Western countries, however, are accustomed to intervention policies, maintaining that a country unable to fulfill its obligations in accordance with accepted mainstream standards shall be subject to international arbitration. Regarding different values as the fundamental responsibility, China and the West often blame each other in a process of interference and anti-interference.

At the level of limited responsibility, the disagreement centers on conflicting standards for judging China's national strength. Western countries define China's international responsibilities based on China's overall national strength. In the eyes of Western countries, China is already the second-largest economy in the world and should shoulder corresponding external responsibilities, including paying more membership contributions to international organizations, increasing foreign aid, taking part in more peacekeeping operations, and fulfilling more carbon emission reduction obligations.

However, most Chinese believe that China would have to undertake undue responsibilities if the total size of China's national economy is to be the only standard for measuring China's national strength. A sense of crisis dating back to the colonial era is still shaping the self-identity of the intellectuals and the general public in China. Chinese people like to look back on the days before the Opium War, when China's total GDP ranked first in the world but was easily defeated by the British Expeditionary Force. The humiliation of being a large but weak country is deeply ingrained in the minds of the Chinese people. Many Chinese hold that China is not yet a superpower because its per-capita GDP ranks only around the hundredth in the world. Many people even question China's history of tightening its belt during economic difficulties while providing foreign aid. The self-reflective sentiment of isolationism was clearly demonstrated when China's total GDP surpassed Japan's to rank second in the world in 2010.

Chinese elites have apparently realized the disparity between Chinese and Western perspectives on China and have begun to reconcile. On one hand, China is not yet a really developed economy; on the other hand, it is obviously a pivotal giant. After the international financial crisis, China has extended its foreign responsibilities in a limited way. The Chinese government has increased aid to Africa and Asia and has canceled certain massive debts of the least-developed countries; Chinese media have proudly reported Chinese relief and medical teams' contributions after the earthquake in Haiti; China has also agreed to increase its contributions to the International Monetary Fund (IMF); China has sent out special envoys to Africa and the Middle East in addition to struggling to maintain the six-party talks; and the People's Liberation Army has sent out warships in the fight against Somali pirates—a rare overseas military operation in over 20 years.

To sum up, with respect to limited responsibility, the Chinese government is indeed undertaking more foreign obligations based on the fact that China's national strength is growing. The Chinese government, however, must reach a balance between external ardency and internal apathy, with more focus on the balance between expanding obligations and rights. Chinese apathy toward Western theory of "Chinese responsibilities" comes not only from a sober judgment about itself but also from a doubt: can China acquire corresponding rights once it shoulders more responsibilities?

Finally, with respect to leadership responsibility, many Westerners wonder whether China will challenge the existing international order. On some levels, a sense of anxiety exists in the West regarding the type of power China will exert on the international stage. That uneasy sentiment is most reflected on the issue of China's growing military power. Western countries have asked China to explain the purpose of newly increased weapons and military expenditure. For the Chinese, the question is self-evident: As an economic power, the country of China feels it too deserves a national defense capability matching that of the United States, Britain, and other countries. The main concentration of the Chinese government and the general public has been on economic development, not militarization, so many Chinese find the question from the West insulting and inimical.

China is also wrestling with its own emotional sense of insecurity. Since the colonial era, China has had a sensitive view of its relation with the West. As China has integrated into the international system, where it has found opportunities for positive growth, fears of seemingly stringent requirements by Western powers have created concerns that the country will not be able to continue to flourish economically.

Chinese sentiment is clearly manifested in the RMB exchange rate issue. The United States has been pressing China in recent years, asking it to revalue its currency against the U.S. dollar so as to "restore the balance of the international trading system."[8] From a rational point of view, Chinese economists and policy makers agree that a more balanced international balance of payments would be more conducive to healthy economic development. To that end, in a few years' time, China has appreciated its currency by 20 percent. There are concerns within China, however, that changing that exchange rate could have negative effects. For example, in the 1980s, Japan acquiesced to Western countries' proposal on the exchange rate issue and appreciated the yen sharply, consequently leading to an economic bubble and putting an end to the country's continuously rising trend of three decades. Many Chinese appeal for watching out for the danger of a Chinese version of the Plaza Accord.

Consensus Between China and the West

Just like in human society, the international community is full of conflicts. Obviously, at the three levels of responsibilities— "fundamental responsibility," "limited responsibility," and "leadership responsibility"—Chinese and Western views of China's international responsibilities often differ. The disparity is caused largely by different values rooted in different historical memories, different national characters, and the present status of these nations.

But what is often overlooked is that at each level, China and the West actually have a considerable degree of consensus: China recognizes the fundamental laws, values, and norms of modern international systems, and the West agrees that China is a country that complies with international rules. China promotes levels of foreign aid and security cooperation according to its growing national strength, carefully maintaining a balance of obligations and rights. China has repeatedly made clear that it is both a beneficiary and a defender of the existing international system, being careful to avoid offending existing international rules. And China has made considerable efforts on the issue of international responsibilities. In those efforts, a hope for greater understanding between the West and China has emerged.

HISTORICAL INFLUENCE OF TRADITIONAL CULTURE

Chinese people have always pursued their historical missions of safeguarding peace, promoting world development, and actively fulfilling the international responsibilities matching their national power. The world—from surrounding neighbors to the countries afar, from economy fields to security fields, and from poverty alleviation to common development—has witnessed China's performance of responsibilities and enjoyed its contributions.

Since ancient times, the Chinese people have believed in harmony and collaboration, emphasizing that a country should show respect to others. They have also valued the spirit of cherishing "men from afar" and "esteeming virtue while restraining force" and have stressed ethical appeal and affinity. Modern China underscores peace, cooperation, and development internationally. As the largest developing country in the world and an active participant in the international community, China has a traditional and contemporary culture, makes diplomatic efforts, and is developing an international identity, all of which have caused the country to become an active player on the world stage as it maintains its sense of responsibility.

China enjoys a rich and profound history and culture, with a philosophical belief in inner gentleness. That ideology reflects itself in China's political ethics, via the pursuit of benevolent rule rather than rule by force. The affinity and attraction of Chinese culture have exerted a gradual and imperceptible influence on the formation of East Asian civilization. In its foreign relations, China has always had an open attitude toward both neighboring countries and distant ones, such as those in Europe. When Marco Polo came to China during China's Yuan Dynasty in the thirteenth century, the court treated him respectfully and gave him an official position. China's close cultural communication with neighboring countries helped in the gradual formation of the Chinese cultural circle, which respected and maintained the values of collaboration, harmony, respect, and trust.

View of Harmony and Collaboration

As the essence of traditional Chinese culture, the concept of harmony and collaboration has directly influenced the country's foreign policy of peace and friendship and shaped its image as a responsible power.

Chinese people advocate natural beauty. Lao Tzu held the view of "harmony between man and nature," saying that "Man takes his law from the Earth; the Earth takes its law from Heaven; Heaven takes its law from the Tao. The law of the Tao is its being what it is."[1] Human beings are part of nature and subordinate to the rules of Tao like everything else, which is coherent with the thought of harmony between humankind and the environment. Chuang Tzu said, "I am born with the universe and coherent with everything," meaning that human beings belong to nature and should be integrated with the universe. The ancient Chinese developed the calendar of 24 solar terms through phenological observations and found that living creatures have natural characteristics of spring birth, summer growth, autumn harvest, and winter storage. They emphasized the views of conformity to the weather and the harmony between human beings and nature. Nowadays, China pays great attention to environmental protection and has taken active measures to promote international efforts for climate change. The country has proactively taken responsibility for carbon emission reduction, creation of a low-carbon lifestyle, and the development of new energy and green products.

The prominent features of traditional Chinese culture are harmony and collaboration. In foreign relations, China believes that all countries should be united and harmonious. Confucius said that "the purpose of respect is for peace." Applying that idea to foreign policy leads to the idea of countries' communicating with one another in peaceful ways instead of resorting to violence. Confucius also believed that "gentlemen seek harmony but not uniformity while the mean persons are in disharmony with each other in spite of uniformity among them."[2] In the same way, countries should maintain their own independence as well as seek common ground while putting aside differences. Confucius held that a person or a country should win others' hearts by virtue and stressed ethical appeal and cultural attraction, saying, "if people in the neighboring countries do not pay homage to you, you attend to the civil development in your own country to attract them, and when they come, you make it so that they would like to settle down and live in peace."[3] Over two thousand years ago, Confucius stated, "Do not do to others what you don't want to be done to you."[4] Today, this saying is praised as the golden rule of relations among nations and is even engraved on the walls of the UN headquarters in New York.

The theory of a harmonious world and other foreign policies advocated by China—such as the policy of peaceful coexistence, good-neighbor relations, seeking common ground and shelving differences, democratization of international relations, diversity of the world, and friendship and partnership with neighboring countries—all stem from the view of harmony and collaboration and contain the rule of moderation and harmony without uniformity. These ideas are profound in content and establish their own system with a universal significance.

Chinese people also advocate an open and tolerant attitude toward foreign cultures, and they are therefore receptive to exchange, absorption, and integration with other countries. For example, when Buddhism, founded in India, was introduced into China during the West Han Dynasty, it spread widely and spawned a great number of classic writings. There had never been a culture as far-reaching, intensively studied, and widespread as Buddhism at the time. In different periods, China also accepted Christianity, Judaism, and Islam with equal treatment and peaceful coexistence. Today's China pursues a free and equal trade policy and currently attracts investments from other countries all over the world.

Since the times of Lao Tzu, Chinese people have believed in the integration of yin and yang, a unity of opposite sides that is separated into two poles and tolerates contradictions. Chinese people insist that this concept be the foundation of harmonious international relations, with the goal of respecting the diversity of cultures and development models throughout the world. Their aim is to promote the spirit of tolerance, equal dialogues, cooperation, and mutual benefit between different cultures and social systems, as well as mutual complementation and introduction between diversified cultures.

Expression of Interests and Righteousness

In relationships with other countries, China follows the principle of giving a lot and taking little, and it focuses on righteousness instead of economic interests. Confucius recognized righteousness as his code of conduct, saying, "For everything in the world, men of honor treat them neither too intimate nor too aloof, just based on the righteousness."[5] He even thought that relying solely on individual interests would lead to hatred and therefore regarded righteousness as a superior value. "A man of honor knows what is right; the mean man knows what is profitable."[6] He also said, "A man of honor treasures righteousness. And with courage and no righteousness, a man of honor will rebel; a mean man will rob."[7] Relations among countries are the same as those among people. Some countries plunder the wealth of other countries for their own economic interests, thereby worsening economic inequality and breaking world harmony.

The concepts of equality and justice derived from the view of interests and righteousness are widely used by China on the world stage. This view of interests and righteousness reflects China's international ideal of "seeking also to establish others if wishing to be established himself and seeking also to enlarge others if wishing to be enlarged himself."[8] China upholds equality and justice in the world arena by generously helping less-developed countries with economic issues and impoverished situations while still overcoming its own economic difficulties. For example, China has built bridges, railways, dams, and factories in Africa to promote local infrastructures and stimulate local economies. It is a Chinese belief that a country can take up its responsibilities fairly, voluntarily, and completely only when it treasures righteousness. China has always maintained a moral uprightness, adhered to its principles, and taken on responsibilities instead of passing the buck, all of which reflect the powerful influence of Confucius's ideas.

In the modern world economy, China has been actively promoting respect for the interests of developing countries, supporting their economic development, and establishing a new international economic system meant to be fair and reasonable. It shows full respect for other countries' interests while protecting its legitimate national interests in order to encourage win-win cooperation and realize mutual benefit. China has developed collaborations with Asian, African, and Latin American countries on the basis of equality by establishing the free-trade area, cutting debts and tariffs, and lifting poverty, resulting in positive social developments. For instance, China has helped establish the Asian Foreign Exchange Reserve of US$120 billion and signed international currency swap agreements of 650 billion RMB; it has written off the debts of 49 heavily indebted poor countries and least-developed countries and provided aid in the amount of 200 billion RMB for other developing countries.[9]

Theory of Benevolent Rule

Benevolent rule is both an idea and a manner of governing a country. Traditional Chinese culture values benevolent rule in that people should be treated with virtue, not ruled by force. It holds that "a happy land run by benevolence" will "satisfy its citizens and attract foreigners,"[10] and hence people can enjoy permanent peace. Confucius said, "What I do not wish men to do to me I also wish not to do to men."[11] So China will never allow other countries' invasion of it, nor will it ever invade others.

Benevolent rule means a peaceful and tolerant culture of antiwar and a view of governance by civilization instead of force. Though there are standing armies in China, they are not frequently used. When they are, they are not for the conquering of territory. The good-neighbor policy is indeed peaceful in its nature. In the Ming Dynasty, Zheng led his huge, fully armed and powerful fleet of thousands westward to spread Chinese culture without any invasions, thereby establishing China's great image and influence.

In foreign affairs, benevolent rule refers to taking into account moral principles in pursuit of national interests. China does not bully weaker countries but cares for their interests; it is against excessive expansion, interference, and use of force, and it tries to resolve conflicts with neighboring countries in a peaceful way.[12] Besides, benevolent rule means affinity. In the powerful Tang and Song Dynasties, China opened up the Silk Road and enjoyed flourishing external economic and cultural exchange. It treated foreign representatives with warm hospitality and respect to show the emperor's affinity.

Since implementation of the reform and opening-up policy, China has embarked on a road of peaceful development. With an independent foreign policy, China will neither form alliance nor seek hegemony. The country pursues a policy of harmony, security, and prosperity toward its neighbors and seeks to solve conflicts in a peaceful and diplomatic way in the world. It will never expand or engage in arms races.

Guiding Ideology of Diplomatic Theories

As a country, China acts as a force of justice to protect peace from big-power politics. Throughout its history, it has experienced great sufferings from wars, poverty, and starvation and gradually became a semicolonial country under the gunboat policy of external powers. With such a historical memory, China understands the importance of peaceful coexistence and sovereign equality between countries. The logic that a country with great power must seek hegemony is contrary to China's history and the Chinese people's will. China therefore neither fears great powers nor bullies weaker ones and has even taken a lead in promising not to be the first to use nuclear weapons during an international conflict.

China has embarked on a road of economic and peaceful development. The theory of peaceful development enjoys popular support at home and has generated widespread praise and trust abroad. All these actions are based on China's diplomatic ideology, and it is those diplomatic concepts of cooperation, security, development, contemporary international cultural understanding, and harmony that directly influence and promote China's behaviors as a responsible power.

Cooperation

After its founding, the People's Republic of China placed great emphasis on cooperation not only with socialist countries like the Soviet Union and parts of Eastern Europe but also with Western countries on the basis of equality and mutual benefit. China has further embraced the concept of international cooperation based on equality, peace, and harmony since introduction of the reform and opening-up policy.

At the seventeenth CPC National Congress, China expressed its wish to "develop friendship and cooperation with all countries on the basis of the Five Principles of Peaceful Coexistence"[13] and never regard any country as an enemy. Instead, the country planned to develop friendships and various levels of partnership internationally—regardless of the social systems and ideologies of other countries or the benefit to its own development. China believes that mutual respect on an equal basis together with cooperation can improve communication, dispel suspicion, and achieve collaborative development. With promotion of the concept of cooperation, China actively fosters regional integration and cooperation between countries as a responsible power.

It has joined in WTO, APEC, G-20, BRICs, the Five Major Developing Nations, ASEAN Regional Forum, IMF, East Asia Summit, Asia-Europe Conference, and other multilateral organizations, playing an active role in all of them. China emphasizes the necessity and possibility of international security cooperation and is involved in the resolution of international disputes. As cooperation and dialogues become the main methods of maintaining regional and global peace, China has made contributions to international peacekeeping operations, international military exchanges and cooperation, nuclear nonproliferation and disarmament, responses to terrorism, the DPRK and Iran nuclear crisis, the Darfur crisis in Sudan, and the Myanmar Crisis. China also pays attention to cooperation with developing countries based on mutual respect and equal consultation to protect developing countries' equal rights of participation in international affairs.

China also develops public diplomacy and extends nongovernmental exchanges. For 60 years, the country's cooperation with others in the world has been pushed forward immensely, and the number of countries having diplomatic relations with China has increased from 18 in the early days of the People's Republic to 171 at present. A favorable situation of "friends all over the world" has taken shape.

Independent Diplomacy

China cherishes its independence—in part due to the challenges it has faced throughout history, suffering from enslavement and occupation. It insists on its own road in spite of external pressure and interference and maintains its responsibility through its own voice, behaviors, and standards, without yielding to other countries' wills. China established its independent diplomatic principles when it was founded, and in the past 60 years it has never changed its stance. Neither in the Cold War, nor at present, and no matter how serious the situation or the pressure China may face, the country always plays an objective, proactive, and fair role in international affairs.

Deng Xiaoping once said: "China's affairs should be handled according to China's situation and by Chinese people. It was, is, and will be our standing point to be independent and self-reliant. Chinese people value the friendship and cooperation with other countries and more the independent rights won through their long-term struggle. Any other countries should not expect China to rely on them and to swallow the bitter fruit of damages to our interests." China will, proceeding from the fundamental interests of the Chinese people and the people of the world, determine its stand and policy in light of the rights and wrongs of the matter itself. China will continue to uphold justice and build its home planet with other countries in the world.[14] As an independent power in the world arena, China is fulfilling its responsibilities.

Security Based on Mutual Trust and Benefit

International security is undergoing profound changes in the world today. The connotation of security is enlarging, with low politics becoming high politics and security issues extending to political, economic, financial, technological, cultural, and other fields in addition to military. Since the 1990s, Chinese leaders have called for the establishment of a new security concept featuring mutual trust and benefit and equality and cooperation internationally, on both bilateral and multilateral occasions.

Mutual trust suggests that countries should transcend the differences of ideology and social systems, cast aside the Cold War and power politics mentalities, and refrain from mutual suspicion and mutual hostility. Countries should instead maintain frequent dialogues and notices on each other's security and defense policies and major operations. Mutual benefit means that all countries should meet the objective needs of social development in the era of globalization, respect one another's security interests and create conditions for others' security while ensuring their own security interests in order to achieve common security throughout.

Equality means that all countries, big or small, are equal members of the international community and should respect one another, treat one another as equals, refrain from interfering in others' internal affairs, and promote the democratization of international relations. Cooperation means that all countries should seek peaceful settlement of their disputes through negotiation and carry out wide-ranging and in-depth cooperation on security issues of mutual concern so as to remove potential dangers and prevent the outbreak of wars and conflicts.

Security is not isolated, zero-sum, or absolute. A country cannot achieve security and stability without achievement of global and regional peace and stability. China should stick to its new security concept featuring mutual trust, mutual benefit, equality, and cooperation; should maintain its security; and should respect other countries' security at the same time to promote the common security of mankind.[15]

With the guidance of the new security concept, China has actively participated in multilateral security dialogues and cooperation, expanded military diplomacy, paid wide attention to global and regional disarmament and arms control issues, and helped in the establishment of a regional security code of conduct. China also stresses strategic dialogues and consultations with other powers and has become a responsible coordinator and mediator of international security affairs. The Shanghai Cooperation Organization (SCO) is a successful case for the application of this new security concept.

Contemporary International Cultural Understanding

After the founding of the People's Republic of China, influenced by domestic political ideology and the international environment in the context of the Cold War, war and revolution became China's themes of the times. Since the 1970s, China's national security situation has changed considerably with the detente between the East and the West and China's integration into the international community, as well as the establishment of diplomatic relations with a large number of countries.

China's leadership gradually realized that war and revolution were not permanent themes to align themselves with as international connectivity and support have evolved. In the 1980s, the leadership drew the conclusion that "peace and development are the two major themes in the current world." Based on those themes, in the past 30 years, China has made continuous efforts to promote world peace and development. In this new period, China has repositioned its view not only in domestic affairs but also in regard to the international community. That view mainly consists of five aspects:

1. Profound changes internationally
2. Construction of a harmonious world
3. Common development
4. Shared responsibility
5. Active participation[16]

As the world continues to undergo major development, changes, and rebalancing, China believes that "the striving for peace and cooperation and the promotion of development are irresistible historical trends" and that the international community should make efforts in building a harmonious world of enduring peace and common prosperity.[17] The interests of countries are interlinked, and they share a common destiny, so they must support promotion of the common development of countries and focus on exchange and cooperation, mutual learning, mutual benefits, and win-win results.

China is a responsible member of the world community, as it always actively participates in international cooperation with other countries against global challenges and threats out of consideration for human existence and development. "The future and destiny of contemporary China have been closely connected with those of the world."[18] "China must combine the independence and the participation in the economic globalization, co-ordinate the domestic and international situations and make contributions to the noble cause of humanity for peace and development."[19]

Concept of a Harmonious World

China has put forward ideas, concepts, and development methods with profoundly Chinese cultural backgrounds during the transformation of the international system in order to narrow the gap between China and the world. China exalts the spirits of democracy, harmony, cooperation, and mutual benefit in international relations. The Chinese people believe that countries should work together on mutual respect and equal consultation for the democratization of international relations in the political field; on cooperation, and complementarities for the balanced and mutual beneficial development of economic globalization in the economic field; on mutual learning, seeking common ground and respecting the diversity of the world to promote the prosperity and progress of civilizations in the cultural field; on mutual trust, enhancing cooperation and insisting on peaceful solutions—instead of wars—to disputes in the world to safeguard peace and stability in the security field; and on mutual assistance and promotion to take care of our home planet in the environmental protection field.[20] China will uphold the spirit of tolerance, protect cultural diversity, and pursue the universal values of peace, development, equality, and justice to realize the progress and security of various cultures and the establishment of a tolerant and harmonious world.

Identities of Big Power's Responsibility

For China, international responsibility is a new subject and an objective requirement from the interaction of internal and external forces. China is undergoing a complicated exchange of interest in a diversified open society of a multilevel structure while maintaining close and frequent communication between domestic and external markets. China is on its way to becoming a responsible stakeholder in the international community because of the status identities of an open society, its role corresponding with national status, its active participation in the international system, and its development of an emerging economy.

An Open Society in the Context of Globalization

China's society has achieved an unprecedented all-directional, multi-angle, and deepened opening up to foreign countries against the background of reform and opening up and globalization. That universally acknowledged progress and achievement have occurred due to the open-world system, free trade, and economic and technological exchanges, as well as China's active participation in the international community. China accepts large-scale international trade and investments, which enhances the interaction between foreign and domestic markets, but the country also continues to protect its own national interests by ensuring the safety of the lives and property of its people, its energy supply, and its ability to expand into overseas markets. By actively undertaking international responsibilities, establishing the international image of a responsible power, and further integrating itself into the process of globalization, China may realize its overseas interests in the context of globalization.

National Roles Under Multiple Identities

China's national role should be considered from both international and domestic points of view. For example, China is the largest developing country in the world, with a population of over 1.3 billion. Its per-capita GDP ranks about 100th. And 254 million Chinese people daily spend less than the latest international poverty line.[21] China's primary responsibilities are to solve the food and clothing problem of so many people in the country and to elevate its people's living standards continuously. In most parts of western China, the economy is underdeveloped and the people live difficult, impoverished lives.

The dual social structure of urban and rural areas is unbalanced, with an obviously extensive mode of economic growth and an unreasonable economic structure. If this one-fifth of the world population mired in chaos, what would China look like? And what would the world look like? Therefore, one of China's responsibilities to the international community is to solve its development problems, which will benefit regional peace, development, and stability. As a permanent member of the UN Security Council, China has prominent political status in the world, which calls for appropriate and proactive international behaviors. It should take on the international responsibilities of a great power and play a prominent role in maintaining regional security and stability and promoting world peace.

After China's participation in UN peacekeeping operations, it has sent a total of 15,603 peacekeepers throughout the world and become one of the most important countries in the UN in contributing peacekeeping troops. Based on the principles of objectivity, justice, and equality, China participates in the coordination of solutions to international hot spot issues and regional security problems, initiated the six-party talks on the DPRK nuclear issue, and continues to work actively for peaceful settlement of the Iran nuclear issue. In addition, as a non-Western emerging-market economy, the China elements have spread to the whole world.

China is enjoying a sustained and rapid economic growth, with a GDP ranking second in the world and a foreign exchange reserve of more than US$1 trillion, ranking first in 2010, which is still growing rapidly. With such increasingly powerful economic strength, China plays a more significant role in the global industrial chain and enjoys corresponding influence and responsibilities. China actively responded to the international financial crisis by sharing the risks and responsibilities of the international market under multilateral frameworks such as G-20 and BRICs. In this way, China has transformed its roles in such multiple and complex identities and performed its international responsibilities corresponding to its strength and abilities in accordance with the principle of "responsibility consistent with power"—neither exaggerated nor minimized.

Participant in the International System

Though China has achieved success in the opening-up process, the country cannot develop further without the rest of the world. It needs a peaceful environment for its development and, in return, will be able to better protect an international environment of peace. China is eager for international peace as much as it is for its own development. China's interests are closely linked with the current international system, and the country has therefore adopted an approach of system improvement instead of destruction. As an important force in maintaining the stability of the international system, China has approached its own development through participation in the international division of labor and by undertaking responsibilities proactively. China has adopted the policy of economic development as a priority and acts as the "model worker" in the international system who develops itself by practical work. At present, China has gone through this approach and will not easily give it up. China has gradually become a significant participant, defender, and builder of the international system.

National Reunification

China is the only power that has not fully realized its unification. The separatism in Taiwan is the biggest obstacle to cross-strait reunification and China's modernization and national rejuvenation. The situation also damages national emotion and dignity. National sovereignty is still in the framework of "one China." At present, and in the near future, one of China's major tasks is to realize national reunification and to make the Chinese people across the strait enjoy reunion, peace, and development together with the rest of the country. Currently, relaxed relations, closer economic exchanges, and deeper interdependence across the Taiwan Strait show a clear trend of coexistence. However, many factors still interfere with those cross-strait political relations, and political and military mutual trust has not been established. Moreover, there are still pro-independence forces in Taiwan. Therefore it remains an arduous task to realize reunification across the strait. And it is a fundamental requirement and the general trend to realize the peaceful development of cross-strait relations and national unity. Only in this way can China really achieve national prosperity, and only based on it can China become a responsible power.

Challenges to Influencing Big Power's Responsibilities

China is a huge country and part of a continent covering an area larger than Oceania and equal to all of Europe. Such a size causes some foreign countries to scrutinize all of China's behaviors and causes nations to be suspicious of China, highlighting and even exaggerating the country's problems. China therefore has to be cautious in the international arena. China also, however, does have problems with which it needs to call for international cooperation and help, such as in health epidemics and climatic catastrophes.

Naturally Endowed Responsibilities

China has a great deal of domestic market and human resources. Its first endowment is the country's enormous population. China has a population of over 1.3 billion, 22 times that of the United Kingdom or France, 10 times that of Japan, and 4 times that of the United States. China ranks first in many demographic indexes.

The second endowment is the country's huge territory. China's land area is about 9.7 million square kilometers, and its ocean area is about 3 million square kilometers. China is therefore responsible for 7 percent of the land on the earth and must manage, govern, and develop the huge territory well. The country has the responsibilities to conserve the biodiversity and marine ecology of the region, along with other aspects of the environment.

China's third endowment is the size of its economy. By the second quarter of 2010, China's GDP ranked second in the world; at the end of June 2010, China's foreign exchange reserve totaled US\$2.5 billion, ranking first. In the first half of 2010, China's total trade volume was US\$1.355 billion. With its unprecedented close economic ties to the outside world, China has an increasing influence on the world economy, and it takes an active attitude toward its responsibilities for world stability and prosperity.

The fourth endowment is China's high rate of dependence on energy. China is rich in various kinds of natural resources, but with high consumption, its foreign dependency rate on oil has reached 51.3 percent.[22] China demands a responsible international market and framework. China's closer foreign economic links to and higher dependency rate on outside countries mean China also needs a safer import channel for trade and energy. China needs to protect the Strait of Malacca, the South China Sea, the Gulf of Aden, the Persian Gulf, and other important marine channels along with necessary international cooperation. Therefore it is natural for China to shoulder its international responsibilities.

Climatic Catastrophes

China is indeed the worst victim of global warming. In the context of global climatic changes, extreme weather events are quite frequent and concentrated in China, such as droughts, floods, storms, mountain fires, extreme heat, and severe cold. It is common for China to have storms and floods in the south and heavy heat and droughts in the north. Glaciers melt and desertification spreads, and the frequency and intensity of disasters are increasing, creating serious economic and property losses and a high death toll. As the global warming problem is related to China's security of energy, food, and climate, China has recognized the necessity and urgency of taking part in international climate cooperation and protecting those securities and interests. Therefore, China attaches great importance to the problem of climatic change. China has taken a series of energy-saving measures at home and actively participates in international operations on this global issue. It not only is responsible for its own people but also appeals to the whole world to cope with global climate issues together.

Nontraditional Security Threats

In recent years, China's leadership has focused on nontraditional security threats, such as epidemic outbreaks and terrorism. One of the challenges currently facing societies throughout the world is that the elements of traditional and nontraditional security threats have become intertwined. For example, China's huge population, its poor health facilities and conditions in rural areas, and its imperfect urban public health system are susceptible to epidemics, such as SARS, H5N1 avian influenza, hand-foot-mouth disease, and AIDS. Nontraditional security threats, including pandemic diseases and major public health emergencies, are causing terrible effects on human health and social economic development not only in China but also throughout the world. Because of population flow, global epidemic monitoring faces a serious challenge, and many developing countries are having difficulties with the situation. International cooperation and joint measures toward biosafety concerns must be enhanced for public welfare and social stability.

The international community must also be active in the prevention of, and response to, bioterrorism. China currently faces terrorist threats from East Turkistan separatist forces attempting to achieve their ulterior purposes through murder and bloodshed. The "7·5" event in 2008 exposed the nature of this terrorism.

China calls for international cooperation to solve nontraditional security problems and aims at reducing threats to the minimum. Its proactive actions reflect its responsibilities and care for human life.

CHINA'S EFFORTS FOR PEACE INTERNATIONALLY AND DOMESTICALLY

As one of the founders of the United Nations, China has witnessed the UN's significant contributions to world peace during the past 65 years. Honoring the fundamental principles of the Charter of the United Nations, China has demonstrated its willingness to assume more responsibility for protecting world peace and to play an increasingly crucial role in participating in world affairs, in settling regional conflicts, and in preserving global stability. China has been driven by its recognition of its own responsibility and its desire to contribute to world peace. Not only does China assist developing countries to boost the economy and stabilize their domestic situations, but it also proactively strives for a fair and just international environment by strongly opposing nuclear proliferation and terrorism and advocating peaceful negotiations as the proper way to address global issues, such as the nuclear crises in the DPRK and Iran. Through these efforts, China has received high praise and respect from the international community.

The West has also noticed the rapid economic development in China as well as the radical changes in the relations between China and the outside world. On one hand, the West has concerns that China may exert impact on the current international orders as other great powers did when they rose. On the other hand, these countries also expect China to be one of the key members in the world arena.[1] Overall, to the people of China, it seems that the Western world is deeply concerned with China's efforts for peace.

Currently, some observers say China is so powerful on the global stage that its actions and decisions will reach deeply into every country on the planet.[2] Without China, many major issues in the world will remain in the air. On hot spot issues such as the DPRK nuclear program, Iran's nuclear program, the Darfur crisis, and the chaos in Myanmar, some Western countries exaggerate China's responsibilities and urge China to pressure certain parties concerned, which has contributed to a growing tension in the international community. It has been argued that such actions are attempts to impair the long-existing friendship between China and certain nations. In addition, Western countries have pressured China to impose sanctions on what have been considered rogue states. If China refuses to do so, there is a fear that it will be blamed as irresponsible. Independent from such requests, however, China has made great contributions to regional security and stability based on fair, objective, and equal principles, which have won applause worldwide.

It has also been proposed that China seems to ignore its duties while asking for more rights on the international stage. From the Western perspective, since the world has endowed China the rights to safeguard security and stability and global responsibilities in the predominant global system, then China has to help solve problems worldwide. For example, in the Darfur crisis, Western countries claimed that China was not exerting "enough influence" on the Sudanese government. And when it comes to nuclear tensions in the DPRK and Iran, Western nations have criticized China for not taking or supporting any further economic or military sanctions. Some claim that China should be responsible for the proliferation of nuclear weapons, technology, and experts.[3] Nevertheless, China has made considerable efforts in tackling the Darfur crisis by dispatching special representatives and mediating among the parties. Always sticking to the nuclear nonproliferation policy, China firmly defends the international nuclear nonproliferation system and promotes global nuclear disarmament. China supports global and regional peace and will not jeopardize people's well-being or the national stability of the countries concerned, not to mention friendly relations with other countries.

China actively participates in UN peacekeeping missions and humanitarian aid, which significantly enhances local security and stability, especially in such areas as Africa, the Middle East, and Haiti.

For example, from Africa's perspective, China is an old and trusted friend.[4] In the multilateral international arena, China strives for justice and equality for developing countries. Moreover, China either lowers its tariffs, or exempts, or reduces debts, and it provides preferential interest-free loans without any preconditions attached for developing countries. Consequently, many developing countries, including members of Group 77, expect China to play an active role in safeguarding the principle of sovereign equality and promoting multilateralism and democratization of international relations.

With a focus on military transparency, China discloses the latest information about its national defense policies, military expenditure, and army buildup and weaponry development through various white papers, including China's National Defense and Arms Control and Disarmament. These actions enhance mutual trust, dispel suspicion, and win wide appreciation and well-intentioned responses from the international community.[5] Among developed countries, China's efforts for peace and security also win high praise. Robert Zoellick, former U.S. deputy secretary of state, spoke highly of China's role as a "responsible stakeholder." Bates Gill, Freeman Chair in China Studies of the Center for Strategic and International Studies, said China is becoming a responsible stakeholder, demonstrating increasing willingness to contribute to international public goods, including economic stability and growth, nonproliferation, and regional security.[6] The renowned Stockholm International Peace Research Institute also has initiated several research projects on subjects like "China and global security," "China's increasing role in peacekeeping," and "China's role in Africa in terms of security."[7]

Chinese Blue Helmets Come for Peace

Since 1948, the UN has performed 63 peacekeeping missions, with 15 ongoing operations involving more than 110,000 peacekeepers. Furthermore, the UN is conducting 12 peace-building operations in order to prevent conflicts and enhance peace and reconstruction.[8] As a permanent member of the UN Security Council, China shoulders responsibilities to safeguard world peace and devotes operations to promote humanity. All of this represents the vision, initiative, and image of a responsible power. Since 1990, China has engaged in several peacekeeping operations and dispatched military observers to UN mission areas such as Cambodia, Haiti, the Democratic Republic of the Congo, Lebanon, Liberia, and Bosnia-Herzegovina. These UN peacekeeping operations act like a mirror reflecting the historical changes of China's role in global issues.

After China recovered its seat in the UN in 1971, it has been actively participating in multilateral diplomacy, which led to changes in its diplomatic views. As for the UN peacekeeping missions, China used to question their effectiveness, contending that the operations could not solve these world problems and would only serve the interests of larger, more developed countries. However, now China sees the missions in a different light. Although peacekeeping operations cannot eradicate all problems, they still can ease tensions and be conducive to local people. In October 1984, China's representative at the Special Political Commission of the UN General Assembly proposed the following seven principles:

1. China supports peacekeeping operations under the principles of the UN Charter.
2. Peacekeeping operations must be made by the parties' request or agreement and strictly respect the country's independence, sovereignty, and territorial integrity.
3. Parties should cooperate with peacekeeping efforts to seek early solution.
4. The permissions of each peacekeeping mission must be clearly defined and may not be used for personal gain or to interfere in internal affairs.
5. Peacekeeping operations must be authorized by the Security Council.
6. Countries should carry their fair share for the costs of peacekeeping operations and for the principle of reasonable burden.
7. Peacekeeping operations must be strengthened, formulating guidelines or taking practical measures as necessary;

peacekeeping operations are an effective way to maintain global peace and security.[9]

Since that time, China has reached a number of milestones in its peacekeeping efforts, including the following:

- **May 1986:** The on-the-spot observation in Middle East with United Nations Truce Supervision Organization (UNTSO) made China aware of the positive influence of peacekeeping operations.
- **September 1988:** China officially applied for a place on the Special Committee on Peacekeeping Operations (SCPO).
- **April 1989:** China became a member of the SCPO. The facts had proved convincingly that the SCPO had become an effective mechanism in realizing the purpose of the Charter of the United Nations and an integral part of its effort in finding a political settlement for region conflicts.[10]
- **April 1990:** China dispatched five military observers to the UNTSO in Pakistan for the first time, a milestone in its participation in the UN peacekeeping operations.
- **April 1992:** China sent 47 military observers and a 400-person peacekeeping engineering detachment to Cambodia at the request of the UN secretary-general. It was the first Blue Helmet troop from China.
- **May 1997:** China agreed in principle to participate in the UN Standby Arrangements System (UNSAS).
- **January 2000:** China sent civil police to carry out special tasks for the United Nations Transitional Administration in East Timor (UNTAET), which was the first time China sent out police for peacekeeping purposes.
- **January 2001:** Chinese civil police conducted peacekeeping missions in Bosnia-Herzegovina, which marked the first time China dispatched peacekeeping civil police to regions outside Asia.
- **December 2001:** China officially set up the Peacekeeping Office in the Ministry of Defense so as to organize and

coordinate China's participation in UN peacekeeping operations.

- **February 2002:** China formally joined the Class-A standby arrangements of the UN.
- **October 2002:** A plan for establishing the UN peacekeeping standby forces was approved by the State Council and the Central Military Commission.
- **April 2003:** China sent out a 175-person engineering company and a 43-person medical unit to the Democratic Republic of the Congo. It was the first time China sent peacekeeping troops to Africa.
- **July 2003:** China dispatched 558 troops to Liberia, which is by far the largest Chinese military contingent in a peacekeeping mission to date.
- **2004:** China sent out a total of 59 civil policemen to East Timor, Liberia, Afghanistan, Serbia and Montenegro, and Kosovo.[11]
- **September 2004:** China received a UN medal for its contributions to peacekeeping operations.
- **October 2004:** China sent a 125-person antiriot police force to the UN Stabilization Mission in Haiti. Before that, China had never sent any troops to UN peacekeeping-mission areas in America. It was also the first time China dispatched a full unit of antiriot forces to carry out peacekeeping missions and to enter a country without diplomatic relations.
- **April 2006:** China sent a 182-person engineering battalion to the UN Interim Force in Lebanon, carrying out tasks including construction, mine clearance and disposals of explosives and offering humanitarian aid to local civilians.
- **May 2006:** China deployed 435 troops to UN peacekeeping forces in Sudan.
- **July 2007:** China, authorized by the UN, increased its troops in Darfur to 315, which was the first UN peacekeeping force entering the region.

- **August 2007:** The UN appointed Major General Zhao Jing-min of China as force commander of the UN Mission for the Referendum in Western Sahara (MINURSO). He was the first Chinese appointed as force commander in the peacekeeping operations.
- **June and July 2009:** China and Mongolia performed a joint peacekeeping exercise, coded Peacekeeping Mission-2009,"which was the first joint peacekeeping operation that China had held with another country.[12]

China's peacekeeping troops have proved to be dependable at critical moments. In Cambodia, 800 Chinese sappers reconstructed roads totaling 500 kilometers long and 36 bridges. They also restored two airports and built barracks covering thousands of square meters. It took the Chinese engineering battalion only three days to complete the road linking the peacekeeping base and the airport in Sudan, one of the hottest places in the world. In the Democratic Republic of the Congo, Chinese forces needed merely 20 days to turn a deserted hill into an ordered military camp. In Liberia, Chinese transport companies successfully accomplished all tasks assigned by the United Nations Mission in Liberia (UNMIL), offering services nationwide and transporting more than 50 thousand tons of cargo of various kinds a length of more than 2 million kilometers without any accident. A senior official from UNMIL spoke highly of Chinese transport companies: "We are carried forward by the wheels of Chinese transport companies."[12b]

In Lebanon, Chinese peacekeeping engineering companies went all out to finish every task. During the Lebanon-Israel clash, they calmly and decisively analyzed the situation and stood up to the challenge, which received high praise from the international community. In Haiti, Chinese peacekeeping police left an outstanding impression, being disciplined and friendly. Also, Chinese peacekeepers will risk their lives if needed: In January 2010, eight peacekeeping staff died in Haiti during the earthquake. They had devoted themselves to UN peacekeeping operations.

China always sticks to the three widely recognized principles of the UN in its peacekeeping tasks: with consent of the parties; impartiality; and nonuse of force except in self-defense and defense of the mandate.[13] Meanwhile, Chinese peacekeeping operations have added their own features based on their perspective about peacekeeping and its diplomatic principles. First, China will not join peacekeeping operations led by any entity other than the UN. China believes peacekeeping operations should be carried out in accordance with the Charter of the United Nations. China also underlines that the UN Security Council takes the pivotal responsibility of preserving world peace; every peacekeeping operation should be authorized by the UN Security Council, which is the best way to demonstrate the UN's leadership and authority in global affairs. Peacekeeping operations should never be deployed recklessly and should never get involved in the conflict. Furthermore, double standards shall never be applied when arranging and carrying out peacekeeping operations.

Second, China never sends out combat troops. China remains cautious in sending combat troops for peacekeeping missions. China mainly sends military officials, police, and civil officials and focuses on logistics tasks, including construction, medical aid, transportation, mine clearing, and humanitarian tasks such as disaster relief, never engaging in combat missions. By doing so, China has developed an impressive image of a humanitarian power and won respect from local people and the world. Besides, civil police, military observers, engineer companies, and medical units sent by China fill the gap of peacekeeping force structure and significantly contribute to the viability and success of UN peacekeeping operations.

Third, China proactively participates in UN peacekeeping operations. China has joined UNSAS and the Class-A standby arrangements. In October 2002, the State Council and the Central Military Commission approved a plan for taking part in the establishment of the UN peacekeeping standby detachment, which means that China can send an engineering battalion, a medical care detachment, and two transport companies at the UN's request.[14] At the same time, China responds swiftly to the request of the UN according to its own realities. At the demand of the countries concerned and the request of the UN Security Council, China usually makes a positive move. This is regarded as a noble responsibility and the capability of a power to undertake its peacekeeping tasks.[15]

There is no denying that China's participation strengthens UN peacekeeping operations. In the past 20 years, China has joined 23 peacekeeping missions and dispatched more than 15,000 peacekeeping troops, military observers, and civil police, 16 of whom sacrificed their lives. Chinese peacekeeping forces have constructed and maintained roads of 80,000 kilometers, built 230 bridges, demolished 8,700 explosives such as mines, transported cargo of 430,000 tons over 7 million kilometers, and provided medical care for 60,000 people. Moreover, as a developing country, China supports UN peacekeeping operations financially and has increased its share of the peacekeeping funding. In 2010, China accounted for nearly 4 percent, or approximately US$300 million,[16] of UN peacekeeping funding, almost 45 times that in 1990, ranking seventh among contributors.[17]

Table 3.1 and Table 3.2 detail China's participation in peacekeeping operations.

Since 2001, China has been increasing its financial contributions to UN peacekeeping operations, which demonstrates China's initiatives and determinations and greatly promotes the UN. In addition, the number of peacekeepers sent by China has witnessed a surge since 2003. By June 30, 2010, there were 2,012 police officers, officials, and soldiers engaged in 11 UN peacekeeping operations, serving as military observers, representative officials, officers, and sappers. Now, China ranks fourteenth among UN members and ranks the top among the five permanent members of the UN Security Council in terms of number of peacekeepers, as shown in Table 3.3.

Figure 3.1 shows the number of peacekeepers sent abroad by China from 2001 to 2010 on UN operations, demonstrating great growth over 10 years.

Table 3.1 China's Current Participation in UN Peacekeeping Operations

The United Nations Truce Supervision Organization	UNTSO	1948.5	5	Truce supervision and disengagement
The United Nations Interim Force in Lebanon	UNIFIL	1978.3	344	Truce supervision and disengagement
The United Nations Mission for the Referendum in Western Sahara	MINURSO	1991.4	7	Peacekeeping mission of sole responsibility
The United Nations Organization Stabilization Mission in the Democratic Republic of Congo	MONUC	1999.11	234	Truce supervision and disengagement
The United Nations Mission in Liberia	UNMIL	2003.9	584	Integrated peacekeeping operations
The United Nations Operation in Côte d'Ivoire	UNOCI	2004.4	7	Integrated peacekeeping operations
The United Nations Stabilization Mission in Haiti	MINUSTAH	2004.6	16	Integrated peacekeeping operations
The United Nations Missions in Sudan	UNMIS	2005.3	466	Integrated peacekeeping operations
The United Nations Integrated Mission in Timor-Leste	UNMIT	2006.8	26	Peacekeeping mission of sole responsibility
The United Nations/ African Union Mission in Darfur	UNAMID	2007.7	324	Integrated peacekeeping operations
The United Nations Organization Stabilization Mission in the Democratic Republic of Congo	MONUSCO	2010.7	—	Integrated peacekeeping operations

Source: The UN Peacekeeping Operation website, before June 30, 2010, http://www
.un.org/chinese/peace/peacekeeping/pastops.shtml.http://www.un.org/en/peacekeeping
/contributors/2010/june10_3.pdf.

Table 3.2 China's Past Participation in UN Peacekeeping Operations

The United Nations Transition Assistance Group	UNTAG	1989.4– 1990.3	Peacekeeping mission of sole responsibility
The United Nations Iraq-Kuwait Observation Mission	UNIKOM	1991.4– 2003.10	Truce supervision and disengagement
The United Nations Advance Mission in Cambodia	UNAMIC	1991.10– 1992.3	Peacekeeping mission of sole responsibility
The United Nations Operation in Mozambique	ONUMOZ	1991.12– 1994.12	Integrated peacekeeping operations
The United Nations Observer Mission in Liberia	UNOMIL	1993.9– 1997.9	Peacekeeping mission of sole responsibility
The United Nations Mission in Bosnia Herzegovina	UNMIBH	1995.12– 2002.12	Peacekeeping mission of sole responsibility
The United Nations Observer Mission in Sierra Leone	UNOMSIL	1998.7– 1999.10	Peacekeeping mission of sole responsibility
The United Nations Transitional Administration in East Timor	UNTAET	1999.10– 2002.5	Integrated peacekeeping operations
The United Nations Mission in Sierra Leone	UNAMSIL	1999.10– 2005.12	Truce supervision and disengagement
The United Nations Organization Stabilization Mission in the Democratic Republic of the Congo	MONUC	1999.11– 2010.6	Truce supervision and disengagement
The United Nations Mission in Ethiopia and Eritrea	UNMEE	2000.7– 2008.7	Truce supervision and disengagement
The United Nations Mission of Support in East Timor	UNMISET	2002.5– 2005.5	Peacekeeping mission of sole responsibility
The United Nations Operation in Burundi	ONUB	2004.6– 2006.12	Integrated peacekeeping operations

Source: The UN Peacekeeping Operations website, http://www.un.org/chinese/peace/peacekeeping/pastops.shtml.

Table 3.3 Ranking of the Permanent Members of the UN Security Council in Terms of Numbers of Peacekeepers

The Perma-nent Members of the UN Security Council	Military Personnel	Peace-keep-ing Police Officers	Total	Ranking
China	1,959	53	2,012	1
France	1,605	96	1,701	2
Russia	362	2	364	3
The United Kingdom	245	36	281	4
The United States	78	11	89	5

Source: The UN Peacekeeping Operations website, before June 30, 2010, http://www.un.org/en/peacekeeping/contributors/2010/june10–2.pdf.

Figure 3.1 Total Peacekeepers Sent by China from 2001 to June 2010

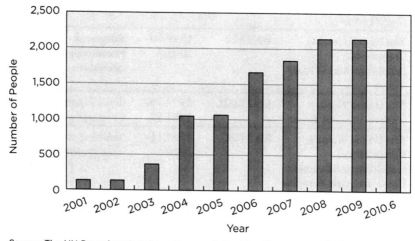

Source: The UN Peacekeeping Operations website, http://www.un.org/en/peacekeeping/contributors.

Chinese medical units, combining modern technologies with traditional Chinese medicine, have excellent skills and equipment. Compared with peacekeepers from some of the traditional peacekeeping countries, Chinese peacekeepers have never been involved in any scandal and do not join the peacekeeping operations for money. China has won respect from the international community through its contributions to preserving world peace and the progress of human beings. UN secretary-general Ban Ki-moon highlights the contributions China has made to the UN peacekeeping operations.[18] Jean-Marie Guéhenno, under-secretary-general of peacekeeping operations, praised Chinese peacekeeping forces in the Democratic Republic of the Congo as an embodiment of the Charter of the United Nations. Liberian president Ellen Johnson Sirleaf underlined that the Chinese peacekeeping force was a strong, disciplined, well-trained, and highly professional troop and was the envoy of the friendship of the Chinese people and the Chinese army. All the Chinese Blue Helmet troops have received UN peace medals. They are not only safeguarding world peace but also promoting friendship and cultural exchange.

China's participation in peacekeeping operations strengthens international cooperation in security. China enhances exchanges with peacekeeping troops from other countries, carries out joint exercises, and sends military officials to participate in professional trainings in UN peacekeeping operations. Through these actions, China put its new security concept in practice, stimulating international cooperation by sharing responsibilities and responding coordinately.

Promoting Global Nuclear Nonproliferation

Since the first atomic bomb detonated in 1945, nuclear threat, like the sword of Damocles, has been hanging over the world. Under the pressure of destructive nuclear weapons, people have been trying to terminate nuclear weapons and reach denuclearization. China is actively engaging itself in the multilateral negotiation on nuclear nonproliferation and honoring the Treaty on the Non-proliferation of Nuclear Weapons. China is playing an important role in denuclearization, the nonproliferation of nuclear weapons, nuclear disarmament, and the peaceful use of nuclear energy, demonstrating its sense of responsibility for humankind.

Global Nuclear Situation Is Still Severe

To master the destructive power, the deterrent, and the political powers of nuclear weapons, a few countries, in pursuit of definite national security, are proactively developing nuclear power. Certain regional security issues—such as conflicts between India and Pakistan, the confrontation between the United States and the DPRK, and between the DPRK and the Republic of Korea—have exerted impact on nuclear arms control and nuclear disarmament. Terrorism has its influence on global nuclear security as well. Some terrorists are searching for nuclear materials or even nuclear weapons.[19]

The nuclear situation is more intense in Asia, especially East Asia. With nine nuclear countries in the world, five of them are located in Asia. Russia and the United States also have nuclear capabilities and have been providing a nuclear umbrella for Japan, the Republic of Korea, and some countries in Southeast Asia. Besides the five Asian nuclear powers—China, India, Pakistan, Israel, and the DPRK—an increasing number of countries possess abilities to develop nuclear programs. There is a greater possibility that terrorists may have access to nuclear specialists and nuclear resources due to globalization, cyberization, the spread of information, the international flow of personnel, and global smuggling.

Currently, some developed countries emphasize only nuclear *nonproliferation*, ignoring the importance of nuclear *disarmament*, implementing double standards in nonproliferation. On one hand, they increase nuclear energy exports to present or future allies, strengthen cooperation on nuclear development with allies, and let them develop nuclear weapons or nuclear technologies, which greatly increases the risk of dissemination of nuclear technologies and materials. On the other hand, they ask other countries to honor the Treaty on the Nonproliferation of Nuclear Weapons. Their behaviors undermine the ethic foundation of the international nonproliferation system. Some Western powers threaten those countries with force or threaten to use force. Under such pressure, these countries tend to develop nuclear weapons to fight against potential containment and threats, only intensifying proliferation.

China's Stands and Efforts in Denuclearization

As one of the permanent members of the UN Security Council and the five nuclear weapon states, China, in support of the complete elimination of nuclear weapons, has adopted a policy of no first use of nuclear weapons and pledges that it will never use or threaten to use nuclear weapons against non-nuclear-weapon states and non-nuclear-weapon regions. Never will it participate in nuclear arms races in any manifestation. China will continue to promote global nuclear disarmament but maintain its minimum nuclear forces to preserve its national security. China consistently promotes nuclear disarmament in order to preserve global strategic balance and stability and believes that all states, nuclear or nonnuclear, should honor the Treaty on the Non-proliferation of Nuclear Weapons. China also promises to never pursue the permanent ownership of nuclear weapons.

China believes that the country that owns the largest nuclear arsenal should reduce its nuclear weapons by a large margin in real terms before any other countries do, respecting the Comprehensive Nuclear-Test-Ban Treaty, so that the Comprehensive Nuclear-Weapon-Ban Convention can be concluded. Nuclear deterrent policy based on using nuclear weapons first should be abandoned so as to reduce the nuclear weapons threat. All nuclear weapons states should make an explicit commitment not to use or threaten to use nuclear weapons against non-nuclear-weapon states or regions and reach an international treaty in this regard with legally binding force.

China also consolidates the international nonproliferation mechanism to prevent the spread of nuclear weapons. All states should accede to the Treaty on the Non-proliferation of Nuclear Weapons to strengthen the safeguards and supervision function of the International Atomic Energy Agency (IAEA). All states should fulfill their duty of nonproliferation and also improve their nonproliferation export control without double standards. China respects every country's right to utilize nuclear energy in a peaceful way and promotes international cooperation. The country also strives for nuclear security in order to reduce nuclear risks. States should abide by international laws related to nuclear security and take effective measures to ensure the safety of their nuclear facilities and materials. The international community should enhance cooperation to fight against nuclear terrorism.[20] China believes that a peaceful and stable international environment can diminish the motivation to develop or possess nuclear weapons. Sticking to the new security concept, which features mutual trust, mutual benefit, equality, and coordination, China notes that we should resolve international conflicts through peaceful measures and should increase the sense of security of states instead of resorting to sanctions, force, and threat.[21]

Since the 1960s, China has proposed to ban and destroy nuclear weapons completely. China has also played a constructive role in addressing nuclear issues in the DPRK and Iran.

Domestically, China sticks to the policy of nuclear nonproliferation. China will not support, encourage, or engage in spreading nuclear weapons, nor will it help other countries develop nuclear weapons, provide assistance for nuclear facilities without IAEA safeguards, export nuclear materials, or conduct exchanges of expertise and technologies with facilities or countries.[22]

In 1997 and 1998, China issued the Regulations on Nuclear Export Control of the People's Republic of China and the Regulations of the People's Republic of China for Export Control on Nuclear Dual-Purpose Goods and Related Technologies, respectively, to perfect the legal system of export controls and strengthen the control of nuclear exports. China adheres to the principles of nuclear export. The principles are as follows:

- All exports should be used exclusively for peaceful purposes.
- All exports should be subject to IAEA safeguards.
- No exports should be retransferred to a third country without prior Chinese approval.

- No uranium should be enriched to over 20 percent without prior Chinese approval.[23]

China attaches great importance to controls on exports of sensitive dual-use technologies and products and upgraded a series of regulations concerning controls on exports of nuclear, biological, chemical, and missile technologies. Criminalizing nuclear terrorism is conducive to the protection of China's nuclear materials and facilities. It will also increase levels of cooperation in antiterrorism between China and other countries to jointly combat nuclear terrorism.

On the international level, China has joined in every international treaty and international organization related to nuclear nonproliferation and strengthened its cooperation and exchanges on the international export control mechanism. Since its entry into the IAEA in January 1984, China has been performing its duty of nuclear nonproliferation as stipulated in the IAEA statute and actively engages in activities that aim at promoting peaceful use of nuclear energy and enhancing supervision, including the following:

- **1985:** China declared it would, of its own will, submit its civilian nuclear facilities to IAEA safeguards.
- **September 1991:** China declared it would report to the IAEA any export to or import from non-nuclear-weapon states concerning nuclear materials of one effective kilogram or more.
- **March 1992:** China acceded to the Treaty on the Non-proliferation of Nuclear Weapons.
- **February 1993:** China voluntarily pledged it would offer the IAEA access to all of its information about imports and exports of nuclear materials, its nuclear facilities, and its exports of relevant nonnuclear materials.
- **May 1996:** China undertook that it would not provide assistance for nuclear facilities without IAEA safeguards, let alone nuclear exports or any exchanges and cooperation of expertise and technologies.

- **September 1996:** China became one of the first signatory countries of the Comprehensive Nuclear-Test-Ban Treaty.
- **October 1997:** China entered the Zangger Committee, one of the mechanisms committed to international nuclear exports controls.
- **December 1998:** China signed the additional protocol related to IAEA safeguards.
- **March 2002:** the additional protocol was approved domestically, first among nuclear-weapon countries.
- **June 2004:** China joined the Nuclear Suppliers Group.[24]

China attended the first Summit on Nuclear Non-proliferation and Disarmament in September 2009 and the multilateral security summit among 47 countries and related international organizations in April 2010. China demonstrated its constructive attitude toward global affairs concerning nuclear issues and played an important role in promoting international cooperation in those two meetings, actively expressing its opinions and engaging in discussions. China keeps a good nuclear security record and takes effective measures to ensure nuclear security. In addition to ratification of the Convention on the Physical Protection of Nuclear Material and the drafting of the International Convention for the Suppression of Acts of Nuclear Terrorism, China supports and participates in technologic cooperation arranged by the IAEA.

Denuclearization on the Korean Peninsula

The DPRK nuclear issue is a very important one on China's diplomatic agenda. According to incomplete statistics, the DPRK nuclear issue was mentioned in 213 regular press conferences held by the Ministry of Foreign Affairs of China (Table 3.4), through which China explained its standpoint and views, advocating a peaceful way to achieve denuclearization on the Korean Peninsula.

Since the late 1950s, the DPRK has been researching nuclear technologies. After decades, its researchers have achieved some progress. The DPRK nuclear issue has consisted of two stages. In the first stage,

Table 3.4 The Times of the Regular Press Conferences by the Ministry of Foreign Affairs of China Which Mentioned the DPRK Nuclear Issue, 2003–2010

Year	2003	2004	2005	2006	2007	2008	2009	2010	Total
Times	71	46	12	8	24	11	32	9	213

Source: "China's Stand on the DPRK Nuclear Issue," http://news.xinhuanet.com/ziliao.

the United States and the DPRK carried out direct dialogues. Conflicts remained on topics such as verification of DPRK nuclear facilities and U.S. financial compensations. In the early 1990s, based on satellite data, the United States suspected that the DPRK was developing nuclear weapons and claimed that it would conduct verification of DPRK nuclear facilities. Meanwhile, the DPRK stated that it did not intend to, nor was it able to, develop nuclear weapons, and it criticized the United States for deploying nuclear weapons in the Republic of Korea. Since then, communications between the two often came to a deadlock, with both sides arguing about the declaration about nuclear activities and sanctions against the DPRK.

On March 12, 1993, the DPRK declared to withdraw from the Treaty on the Non-proliferation of Nuclear Weapons for the first time. On October 21, 1994, the DPRK-U.S. Nuclear Agreed Framework was signed between the United States and DPRK in Geneva. The framework stipulated that while DPRK maintained a freeze on its nuclear facilities, the United States would preside over energy development on the Korean Peninsula and construction of light water reactors and would provide heavy oil, which the United States did not deliver in entirety. The situation grew more complicated in the second stage.

Countries including China, Russia, the Republic of Korea, and Japan exerted joint efforts to resolve the DPRK nuclear issue by creating a platform to facilitate multilateral dialogues and negotiations. However, after the United States stopped providing heavy oil, the DPRK, once again declared to withdraw from the Treaty on the Non-proliferation of Nuclear Weapons on January 10, 2003. On October 9, 2006, the DPRK announced it had conducted a successful underground nuclear test. On May 25, 2009, the DPRK declared it had finished a successful nuclear test.[25] At the same time, the DPRK was also developing its ballistic missile capabilities.

To ease the mounting tension, China has actively promoted peaceful dialogues through mediation and shuttle visits. Also, for peace and stability on the Korean Peninsula and in Northeast Asia, China, taking the initiative as a host country, launched the six-party talks with help from various parties to achieve more-common grounds, fewer conflicts, and a consensus as soon as possible. By June 2008, the six-party talks had been convened to the sixth round.[26] The six-party talks have three major tasks:

1. Denuclearization
2. Normalization of relations between the countries involved
3. Discussion about establishment of the Northeast Asia Security Mechanism[27]

The achievement of those three goals is beneficial to the stability of Northeast Asia and will promote prosperity in both East Asia and Asia as a whole.

After the second DPRK nuclear crisis broke out, China began to mediate between the DPRK and the United States. In April 2003, the three-party talks on nuclear issues between the DPRK, China, and the United States were convened. Since then, China has continued to engage in shuttle diplomacy by sending several senior officials around. Soon, the three-party talks evolved to the first six-party talks among China, the DPRK, the Republic of Korea, the United States, Russia, and Japan in August. And the principle of peacefully resolving the DPRK nuclear issue through negotiations was recognized. The DPRK nuclear issue has been taken onto a multilateral track.

In February 2004, the second round of the six-party talks was held in Beijing, hosted by Chinese vice foreign minister Wang Yi. Based on the opinions of all the parties involved, the six parties reached a consensus, which was recorded in the Chairman's Statement. It was the first time that the six-party talks concluded in written form, which then became a regular mechanism. In June 2004, at the third round of the six-party talks, through China's mediation, all parties stressed the need for a step-by-step process for a peaceful solution to the nuclear issue based on a words-for-words and action-for-action principle.

In June and September 2005, the Joint Statement of the Fourth Round was adopted, and six parties achieved six consensuses regarding the DPRK nuclear issue. In 2005, in preparation for the fifth round of the six-party talks, Li Bin, Chinese envoy in charge of Korean Peninsula affairs, made a 13-day visit to the DPRK, the United States, and the Republic of Korea from October 18 to 30. Subsequently, the fifth round was conducted in November 2005, in December 2006, and then in February 2007. During this period of time, the DPRK finished its first nuclear test and announced the disablement of the Yongbyon nuclear facility.

At the same time, other parties agreed to offer economic assistance, energy support, and humanitarian aid to the DPRK. In March and October 2007, after the sixth round of the six-party talks in Beijing, the joint statement was announced. The statement concerns denuclearization on the Korean Peninsula, the normalization of relations between nations concerned, economic and energy aids to the DPRK, and the six-party foreign minister meetings.[28]

Thereafter, since the DPRK bailed out, the six-party talks were suspended. In June 2009, the United Nations Security Council unanimously adopted Resolution 1874, condemning the DPRK for withdrawing from the six-party talks for the second time. China voted for this resolution, which demonstrated China's determination in the denuclearization of the Korean Peninsula. In 2010, with China mediating between the DPRK and the United States, the tension between the two sides greatly decreased. The two sides both were inclined to resume the six-party talks. On the basis of common interests between the DPRK and the United States, China encouraged the two to take action and honor their commitments to promote mutual trust and fortify the foundation for future common ground. When the conversation reached a bottleneck, China actively mediated between the DPRK and the United States, proposed compromise plans, and became a key factor for the progress made in the talks. The international community speaks highly of the positive role China plays in the six-party talks.[29]

China is eager for denuclearization and peace on the Korean Peninsula—more than any country in the world is. So China demonstrates great determination, considerable efforts, and significant contribution to the DPRK nuclear issue, which is in line with China's consistent foreign policies and national interests. Also it shows the image, real actions, and requirements of a responsible power.

Initially, this is in accordance with China's Good-Neighbor Policy. Relations with neighboring counties are priorities in China's diplomacy.[30] China has been emphasizing the promotion of a good neighboring environment and common development through neighboring diplomacy. China treats neighboring countries in a friendly manner and considers them as partners. According to the Good-Neighbor Policy of harmony, peace, and prosperity, the DPRK will always be China's neighbor and traditional friend. So China will continue to actively facilitate the six-party talks through shuttle diplomacy and will work to resolve the DPRK nuclear issue by diminishing conflicts through conversations. Harmony means friendship with the DPRK and being a good neighbor. Peace represents China's efforts in keeping stability on the Korean Peninsula. Prosperity demonstrates China's role as the biggest trade partner of the DPRK, boosting its economy through bilateral cooperation and promoting people's well-being.

Moreover, China's action reflects the principle and the goal of nuclear nonproliferation. On October 19, 2003, on meeting U.S. president George W. Bush prior to the APEC Leaders' summit in Bangkok, Chinese president Hu Jintao stated that China firmly upholds the peace, stability, and denuclearization of the Korean Peninsula and advocates a proper response to the DPRK's reasonable security concerns. Nonproliferation has been China's principle. Due to long-term historical malevolence and the complicated current situation, the Korean Peninsula should stick to the principle of nuclear nonproliferation as well. Meanwhile, it is notable that the United States has already exerted nuclear threat on the DPRK by providing a nuclear umbrella for the Republic of Korea, which will definitely escalate the DPRK's sense of insecurity. Thus, denuclearization on the Korean Peninsula should be a complete one, with no nuclear weapons in any form.

Furthermore, such denuclearization would contribute to China's national security. China is the only country in the world surrounded by nuclear weapons. Northeastern China, which connects to the DPRK, enjoys essential security significance and is an important heavy industrial base with a large population. So a nuclear collision on the Korean Peninsula would surely affect China's security. And it would also undermine the security environment in Northeast Asia, accelerating the arms race and resulting in a nuclear domino effect. That is why a peaceful resolution to the DPRK nuclear issue is imperative to a peaceful and stable Northeast Asia and to all the countries in the region. As a matter of fact, the DPRK nuclear issue concerns not only nuclear weapons but also the security problem on the Korean Peninsula. Because of the confrontation on the peninsula, the DPRK deems nuclear weapons a way to protect its security. Therefore, a peaceful security environment is crucial to solution of the nuclear issue.

Last, denuclearization is in line with China's diplomatic stand of solving crises through peaceful conversations. China considers harmony as its core principle of foreign policy and intercourse, so it believes that peaceful conversation is the best way to address crisis. The six-party talks can resolve the DPRK nuclear issue by providing a forum for various parties to exchange their views. China encourages the stakeholders in Northeast Asia to communicate on a basis of peaceful dialogues and multilateralism instead of threatening the use of, or indeed resorting to, force.

We should solve the problems step by step while seeking common ground and putting aside differences. Secret diplomacy, coalition diplomacy, or bloc confrontation should be replaced by candid talks. We should adopt the mechanism of irregular meetings to create conditions for denuclearization on the Korean Peninsula. Respecting the sovereignty and the territorial integrity of other countries, China actively contributes to regional peace while never interfering with other countries' domestic affairs. China calls for the DPRK and the United States, on the precondition of compromise, to demonstrate their sincerity in order to promote mutual trust. Out of common interests, China is against the use of ideology from any party to impede conversations.[31]

A Peaceful Solution to the Iran Nuclear Issue

In addition to the DPRK nuclear issue, the Iran nuclear issue is a major concern in today's world. The nuclear energy program in Iran can date back to the late 1950s, when Mohammad Reza Shah Pahlavi was in power. At that time, nuclear energy development was supported by such Western countries as the United States, Germany, and France. However, since the end of diplomatic relations between the United States and Iran in 1980, the United States has been questioning the motivation of Irani nuclear energy development and criticizing Iran for developing nuclear weapons under the cover of peaceful utilization of nuclear energy. Then the United States adopted several deterrent policies against Iran. China, based on a sense of responsibility, is also against the development and proliferation of nuclear weapons and is actively engaged in international actions related to the Iran nuclear issue. But China asserts that the Iran nuclear issue should be resolved through peaceful approaches like dialogues and negotiations. Sanctions can only deteriorate well-being rather than solve the problem.

First, China sticks to its principles and upholds the authority of the nuclear nonproliferation regime and the UN Security Council. As a permanent member of the UN Security Council, China consistently supports the international nuclear nonproliferation regime. Therefore, China opposes Iran's ownership of nuclear weapons while recognizing Iran's equal right to peacefully utilize nuclear energy. Also, China advocates for peaceful resolution through diplomacy and negotiations. Since November 2006, the UN Security Council has adopted Resolutions 1737, 1747, 1803, and 1929 concerning sanctions against Iran. In support of the international nuclear nonproliferation regime and of peace and stability in the Middle East, especially the gulf area, China voted for the four resolutions. But China still believes that peaceful dialogues will be more helpful than sanctions. The resolutions the UN Security Council has adopted do not mean that the international community gives up *diplomatic* resolution of the Iran nuclear issue. The purpose of these resolutions is to restart the negotiations on the Iran nuclear issue. That purpose reflects the attitude and concern of the international community toward this issue. And it demonstrates the determination of the international community in seeking a peaceful way to solve this problem.[32]

Second, China deals with relations between the various parties concerned by means of flexibility in an appropriate way. During the process, China maintains in-depth communications with all parties, including Iran. A friendly relationship with Iran will facilitate Iran's integration into the international community and is conducive to regional peace, stability, and development. To promote a peaceful solution to the Iran nuclear issue, China actively participates in foreign minister meetings held between China, the United States, Russia, Britain, France, and Germany. Furthermore, China initiated discussion about resuming negotiations on the Iran nuclear issue during a meeting of the political director generals of the Ministries of Foreign Affairs of those six countries and the director general of external relations of the European Council held in Shanghai and exchanged views on implementation of the consensus reached at the meeting of the foreign ministers from the six countries (Table 3.5).[33]

Third, in adhering to the legitimacy, China protects the legal rights of normal trade. We should not punish normal trade and countries that have regular and legal economic and trade relations with Iran because of the Iran nuclear issue.[34] What is worth mentioning is that

Table 3.5 The Times of Reference to the Iran Nuclear Issue at the Regular Press Conferences of the Chinese Ministry of Foreign Affairs, 2005–2010

Year	2005	2006	2007	2008	2009	2010	Total
Times	3	3	18	13	15	36	88

Source: http://news.xinhuanet.com/ziliao.

some Western media criticize China for not supporting the sanctions against Iran because China wants to protect its energy and commercial interests in Iran. This statement is untenable. China does enjoy great economic interests in Iran. This is regular and legitimate cooperation, which is beneficial for Iran's economy and people. So it is reasonable for China to protect its legitimate legal rights as well as other countries' rights in Iran. Actually, any actions related to the Iran nuclear issue should not interrupt Iranian people's normal lives and the regular economic and trade exchanges between Iran and other countries. The actions should contribute to the momentum of the recovery of global economy.[35] It is evident that China receives praise for its contributions to local people's well-being, economic development through promoting justice, mutually beneficial cooperation, peaceful dialogues, and negotiations.

Fourth, China gives priority to the welfare of 70 million Iranian people based on the people-oriented principle. Energy exports such as oil exports represent the pivotal industry and primary source of foreign exchanges for Iran. The revenues brought by oil represent more than half of the total foreign exchange incomes in Iran. As the pivotal industry in Iran, the energy industry has great influence on the Iranian people's income. The international sanctions should concern only the nuclear nonproliferation field and not the pillar of Iran's economy. Iran has a simple economic structure, and sanctions, especially those related to importation of medicines and medical equipment, would have negative impact on people's living standard and hence result in humanitarian crises, barriers, suspicion, and confrontations. Ultimately, it is the civilians who have to bear the consequences.

China and Iran have enjoyed a friendly relationship for more than 2,000 years. Since ancient times, the two countries have been maintaining close cultural exchanges. Persia served as the strategic area along the Silk Road and was a transit hub for economic and cultural exchange. Those cultural and economic exchanges, blazing their ways through long distance, consolidated the foundation of the friendship between the two countries. Today, there are frequent exchanges in areas like economy, technology, trade, and culture, thanks to friendly relations between China and Iran. Out of friendship, China sincerely calls for a peaceful solution to the Iran nuclear issue. At the same time, China believes that the international community should resort to negotiation instead of force and give Iran a safe environment.

Crackdown on Terrorism

Terrorism—which threatens innocent lives, human dignity, and security—is the public enemy of peace lovers all over the world. Currently, increasingly frequent terrorist activities, such as the September 11 attacks, Bali bombings, London subway bomb attack, and Xinjiang 7·5 incident—severely undermine the security and order of the international community and trample human and humanitarian rights. Therefore, it is our common task to prevent and fight against terrorism. As a responsible power as well as a victim of terrorism, China firmly opposes global terrorism in any manifestation. Domestically, China strengthens its counterterrorism capabilities and takes measures to maintain domestic stability so as to eradicate the roots of terrorism. Internationally, China attaches great importance to global and regional cooperation and maneuvers in antiterrorism. Also China proactively participates in UN joint operations against terrorism.

In terms of antiterrorism, China firmly supports the leadership of the UN. China believes that all operations should comply with the Charter of the United Nations and other acknowledged norms of international law. All actions should be based on valid evidence and have clear objectives. All actions should neither harm civilians nor randomly enlarge the scope of attack. Terrorism exists among a few extremists. So it should not be connected to certain religions or nationalities.[38] Terrorism has always been a major concern on the UN's agenda. The UN has formulated 13 international conventions within its framework. The Security Council has participated in antiterrorism through resolutions and by establishing various affiliated organizations.[39] Meanwhile, many development programs, agencies, and organizations under the UN devote themselves to antiterrorism undertakings. Due to the intensifying cultural and economic interdependence during globalization, only through cooperation instead of unilateralism can we counter terrorism. And only with the leadership of the UN can we achieve cooperation.

Moreover, China is against double standards in antiterrorism. Terrorism is the enemy of the whole international community due to its ruthless harm to lives. The international community should take a concerted and intolerant stand against terrorism in all forms no matter where it takes place or whom it targets.[40] All terrorism is evil in nature. So no country, political party, or organization shall adopt double standards toward terrorism for political reasons or other self-serving purposes. Some countries focus only on their own interests, ignoring the terrorist threats other countries are facing. Such countries have different definitions for terrorist groups, which is counterproductive to international cooperation. Last, China wants the root of terrorism eradicated. At present, the disparity between the South and the North is widening. Owing to the unfair political and economic orders, many developing countries are becoming increasingly marginalized, which leads to the degradation of people's lives there. As a result, a few terrorists will take advantage of that and advocate for terrorism by instigation of emotions. Conflicts and turbulence nourish terrorism, and poverty and underdevelopment give birth to terrorism. To eradicate terrorism, the international community should focus on three areas: easing regional and international tensions, eradicating poverty, and strengthening antiterrorism cooperation.[41] In short, antiterrorism operations should start with the root of terrorism.

China plays an important role in global antiterrorism through accession to international conventions. As early as 2001, China was already entering into several antiterrorism international conventions. After September 11, China supported and implemented the resolutions adopted by the UN and the UN Security Council, such as the International Convention on Stopping Terrorist Explosions and the International Convention on Severing Financial Aid to Terrorism. China also carried out conversations and consultations with countries interested in antiterrorism. As a permanent member of the UN Security Council, China promoted the approval of antiterrorism Resolutions 1267, 1373, 1333, and 1456 in the UN Security Council. After establishment of the Shanghai Cooperation Organization, the Shanghai Treaty on Cracking Down on Terrorism, Separatism, and Extremism was concluded by SCO members to strengthen regional multilateral cooperation and jointly combat terrorism. China Signed the Cooperation Agreement on Tackling the "Three Forces" respectively with Kyrgyzstan, Kazakhstan, Tajikistan, Uzbekistan, and Pakistan in order to exert concerted efforts in fighting against terrorism, separatism, and extremism. The members of the Shanghai Cooperation Organization signed the Decision on the Regional Anti-Terrorist Structure. Then the antiterrorism center in Bishkek, Kyrgyzstan, was established to collect, analyze, and share antiterrorism intelligence.

China has also further improved domestic antiterrorism legislations. On December 29, 2001, the standing committee of the People's Congress approved the Third Amendment to Criminal Law of the People's Republic of China, which criminalized many terrorist activities, added several new crimes related to terrorism, and increased the magnitude of the penalties. The amendment provides powerful legal guarantees for prevention and combat of terrorism.[42] Groups and individuals defined as terrorists are banned from activities in China; their assets get frozen; and they are permitted no support, financial aid, or asylum.

Devote Significant Efforts to the Peace Process in the Middle East

The Middle East is one of the most influential regions in the world. It enjoys an important strategic position, abundant resources, a long history, and splendid culture. But the situation in the Middle East is complicated, with lots of hot spot issues and the risk of wars and terrorism. Various powers are competing for an upper hand in this region. Stability and development in the Middle East are preconditions of global peace and prosperity. For a long period of time, some hot spot issues have lacked fair and reasonable solutions while new conflicts emerge that threaten peace and security in this region. As a responsible power, China proactively engages itself in the peace process in the Middle East. China plays its constructive role in searching for proper solutions to hot spot issues in the Middle East and gulf areas by supporting dialogues and diplomatic and non-confrontational solutions.

Among the political powers, China is the only one maintaining a good relationship with every country in the world. With regard to the Middle East issue, China sticks to its principles and makes decisions according to the rights and wrongs of the matter itself, facilitating communications and preserving peace and stability in the region and in the world as a whole.[43] China believes that all parties should strive to realize regional peace and stability. Wars and force can never be fundamental solutions to problems, so in front of the complex conflicts and disputes, dialogues and consultations on an equal footing should be strengthened and the peace process firmly promoted according to relevant UN resolutions, the land-for-peace principle, the road map-for-peace plan and the Arab Peace Initiative.

Mutual respect should also be upheld. The efforts of the countries in the Middle East to explore their own ways of development according to their national conditions should be respected and guaranteed as the region enjoys its own historical and cultural heritage. A moderate and tolerant spirit should be followed in handling differences among various civilizations in the region. Differences should not become the root of conflicts and disputes but the driving force for learning from one another and for integration in the region.

Cooperation in development should be encouraged as well. Development is an important basis and safeguard for the preservation of peace and the realization of stability, without which a long-lasting peace cannot be achieved. Development should be realized through mutually beneficial cooperation against the background of globalization. Wide regional and global economic cooperation will promote the prosperity of all countries, enhance understanding and friendship among peoples, and be conducive to lasting peace in the region and the world.[44]

China and the Arab countries enjoy a time-honored friendship. Because China and the Arab countries are emerging markets, they have similar standpoints and interests. China is the first country to support Arabic and Palestinian peoples in restoring their legitimate national rights. Since 1949, China has been attaching importance to friendship with Arab countries. In January 1955, China established diplomatic relations with Afghanistan, and on May 30, 1956, with Egypt, marking a breakthrough in China's relations with Arab countries. After that, China developed diplomatic relations with Syria and Yemen. During their struggles against imperialism, the Chinese government and the Chinese people "always stand by the Arab peoples." Then China set up diplomatic relations with more Arab countries, including Syria, Yemen, Iraq, Morocco, Algeria, and Sudan, one after another.

China actively supports the Palestinian people's striving for their national rights. After the reform and opening up, China developed brotherhood with Arab countries and friendly and cooperative relations with Israel. In July 1990 and January 1992, China established diplomatic relations with Saudi Arabia and Israel, respectively. Until then, China had established diplomatic relations and maintained extensive good relations with all countries in the Middle East. On January 30, 2004, President Hu paid a visit to the headquarters of the League of Arab States in Cairo and met Secretary-General Amr Moussa and delegates from 22 member countries. After the meeting, Chinese foreign minister Li Zhaoxing and Moussa launched the China-Arab Cooperation Forum and announced the Communiqué of the China-Arab Cooperation Forum.[45] So far, four ministerial meetings have been convened.

In recent years, in order to accelerate the peace process and demonstrate its concerns on the issue, the Chinese government established the office of the Middle East envoy and sent several envoys to the countries or regions involved for visits and investigations. Also the envoys participate in bilateral and multilateral diplomatic activities to bridge the gaps, which demonstrates China's standpoint in a peaceful resolution of conflicts and which enhances the mutual understanding and friendship between China and countries in the Middle East. So countries in the Middle East in turn attach great importance to China's envoys to the Middle East. In September 2002, Wang Shijie, a senior diplomat, was appointed as the first Middle East envoy and ambassador to Bahrain, Jordan, and Iran. In April 2006, Sun Bigan, a senior diplomat who had been ambassador to Saudi Arabia, Iraq, and Iran, was appointed the second Middle East envoy. Then, in March 2009, Wu Sike, former ambassador to Saudi Arabia and Egypt, succeeded Sun as the third Middle East envoy. All of them specialized in diplomacy in the Middle East and were familiar with Middle East issues. The envoys paid dozens of visits to countries in the region, meeting the relevant national leaders and making significant efforts. They also attended international meetings concerning aid to Palestine and Lebanon, provided assistance according to their abilities, and gained high praise from the international community.

China grasps every chance to promote peaceful conversations among parties concerned in the Palestine and Israel Middle East conflict. In April 2006, President Hu paid a visit to Saudi Arabia and several West Asian countries, which consolidated the friendship between China and the Arab world. China advocated the Riyadh Declaration, which was adopted at the nineteenth Conference of Heads of the League of Arab States in March 2007. In May 2007, Chinese foreign minister Yang Jiechi exchanged in-depth views with foreign ministers and representatives of relevant countries and the secretary-general of the League of Arab States at the enlarged meeting of foreign ministers of Iraq's neighbors and the International Compact with Iraq Conference. Later that year, he also attended the Middle East peace conference held in Annapolis, Maryland, and proposed five points to accelerate the peace process.[46]

These proposals are suitable and feasible, so they receive wide appreciation from the international community. In April 2009, Yang visited Egypt, Palestine, Israel, Syria, and Russia to exchange views on how to address the issue between Palestine and Israel. He noted that both Palestine and Israel should adhere to the principle of establishing two independent countries. Also, when visiting the headquarters of the

League of Arab States in November 2009, Prime Minister Wen Jiabao pointed out that peaceful dialogues and reconciliation, instead of confrontations and violent conflicts, are the fundamental ways to solve the Middle East issue. China is willing to promote a comprehensive, fair, and effective solution to the Middle East issue by deeper communications with Arab states and all parties involved.[47] In January 2010, Foreign Minister Yang visited Saudi Arabia again to make further efforts in promoting the peace process.

Case Study—Humanitarianism in Resolving the Darfur Crisis in Sudan

Located in western Sudan, the Darfur region, with a population of over 6 million people, covers an area of more than 500,000 square kilometers, one-fifth of the total. The region accommodates more than 80 different tribes and ethnic groups and is the most underdeveloped area in Sudan. Due to poverty and limited resources, the region is suffering constant ethnic conflicts and collisions.

As Sudan's friend and a permanent member of the UN Security Council, China has the responsibility to play a constructive role in the appropriate solution to the Darfur issue. On this issue, China has demonstrated its images of peace, development, and cooperation. China sent out special representatives on behalf of the Chinese government and the peacekeeping sappers to provide humanitarian assistance in the region, which actions gained wide praise from the international community. Jean-Marie Guéhenno, the UN's undersecretary-general of peacekeeping operations, spoke highly of China's important and constructive role in seeking common ground on the Darfur issue in the UN Security Council.[48]

China firmly holds a position for peace in addressing the Darfur issue. China, in support of the sovereignty and territorial integrity of Sudan, has been promoting a political solution through dialogues and equal consultations. In February 2007, President Hu noted that the principle of the Chinese government on this issue is to achieve peace, stability, and economic development in Darfur through negotiations on an early date. China respects the sovereignty and territorial integrity of Sudan. The resolving of the Darfur issue is productive to national reconciliation, unity, and peace and stability in the country. China also insists on a peaceful resolution through dialogue and equal consultation. China supports a political solution to the Darfur issue and believes that international organizations such as the African Union and the UN should play constructive roles in the peacekeeping operations in Darfur. The current priorities are stability in the region and the well-being of people there. The most urgent tasks are to achieve a comprehensive cease-fire and accelerate the process of political consultations.[49] China adopts a two-track strategy. First, China emphasizes sending peacekeeping forces to Darfur. Second, China promotes the political process in the Darfur region through peaceful and diplomatic means.

China's stance and policies on the Sudan issue, especially the Darfur issue, are appreciated by the international community such as the African countries, the African Union, and the League of Arab States. China has always adhered to the principles of noninterference in the domestic issues of other countries and provision of aid for Africa without any conditions attached. So it is untenable when some Western media claim that China cooperates with the current Sudanese government, ignoring human rights.

Since 2004, China has sent several special envoys—including senior diplomats Lü Guozeng, Zhai Juan, and Liu Guijin—to Sudan and other countries involved in the conflict. On May 10, 2007, the Chinese government appointed Liu Gui, a senior diplomat, as the special representative in Africa affairs.[50] This was the first position set up in this field, which demonstrates China's increasing concerns in this area and China's willingness to play a more active and constructive role in African affairs. The Chinese representatives met with leaders and many ministers of Sudan several times and visited the Darfur region. They also attended the handover ceremony of the second batch of humanitarian aid to Darfur.

China also has sent peacekeeping forces to Darfur. Since the outbreak of the Darfur crisis in February 2003, more than 200,000 people died directly or indirectly in the armed conflicts, and at least 2 million people became homeless.[51] In 2007, China, as the rotating president of the UN Security Council, facilitated the adoption of Resolution 1769 by the UN Security Council to send out mixed peacekeeping forces to Darfur. In April 2007, Zhai Juan, Chinese assistant foreign minister, encouraged the Sudanese government to accept the three-stage plan. On April 16, 2007, Sudanese foreign minister Lam Akol announced that Sudan had accepted the package plan that the UN and the African Union supported. The international community widely recognized China's key role in this agreement.[52]

In November 2007, China sent a 140-person advance troop to Nyala, the capital of South Darfur, as the first UN peacekeeping force in this region. The main task of the troop was to set up the new camp, 2 kilometers long and 1.5 kilometers wide, in the South Darfur area for the United Nations/African Union Mission in Darfur (UNAMID). In July 2008, the 172 follow-up members of the first Chinese peacekeeping sappers to Darfur arrived. For years, the Chinese peacekeeping forces in Darfur demonstrated their abilities, disciplines, and love for peace. The UN Mission in Sudan highlighted the contributions Chinese peacekeeping forces had made in Darfur with a collective contribution award for the Chinese sappers, transport unit, and medical unit, as well as an individual contribution award for 22 peacekeeping members in September 2007.

China believes that the key to the solution of the Darfur issue is to eradicate poverty, develop the economy, and concentrate on reconstruction and economic recovery in the Darfur region. In order to ease the humanitarian crisis in Darfur and elevate the standard of living, China sent four batches of aid, worth US$10 million, half of which has been already transferred to the region. Later, China decided to send another batch of material assistance worth 40 million RMB. In November 2008, China provided US$3 million for Sudan to promote the unification of the country. In addition, the Chinese government invested nearly US$30 million in the dam construction project in North Darfur. The operation of Chinese petroleum enterprises in Sudan also contributes significantly to economic and social development there, transforming Sudan from a country poor in oil to one with a relatively complete oil industry. China will continue to send prefabricated houses for 120 schools, transportation equipment, generators, water pumps, and other materials needed for recovery and development. In addition, China exempts Sudan's debts and offers Sudan more access to China's market. Furthermore, China sets up agricultural demonstration centers and malaria prevention and cure centers while providing more official development aid and human resource trainings. It is now widely acknowledged that economic and trade cooperation is the best way to solve the Darfur issue.

On February 23, 2010, the cease-fire agreement between the Sudanese government and the major antigovernment organization—the Justice and Equality Movement, was signed in Doha, the capital of Qatar, which put an end to the seven-year armed conflict in the Darfur region. With China's efforts and influence, this monumental document was signed to end the Darfur conflict, marking a crucial step in the peace process in Darfur.

INTERNATIONAL UNDERSTANDING OF CHINA'S DEVELOPMENT

Having experienced long-term underdevelopment and material deprivation, the Chinese people have a special understanding of the word *development*. In their eyes, development is not simply the urgent desire of an individual to go beyond the status quo and pursue a better life; it connotes the collective imagination of China catching up with advanced countries and achieving national rejuvenation. The reason is very simple: China had long been a leader in agricultural civilization before it was placed at the bottom of the international system upon stepping into modern society along with continuing humiliation and defeat for over a hundred years. The Chinese people would regain confidence and find their self-identity only through learning and establishing a modern lifestyle and values and achieve self-renewal of the ancient civilization. In this sense, the connotation of development is not just GDP growth, urbanization, and cement and steel production but, rather, concerns grand transformation of the whole social system to an industrial civilization.

With the progress of reform, China's understanding of development is also deepened. In terms of the concept of governance, China's leaders have gradually come to realize the costs of resource, environment, and society paid for too much emphasis on economic priorities, and so they have put forward a scientific outlook on development to guide China's overall development in the new era. In its foreign policy, China positions itself as a developing country, adheres to the approach of peaceful development, builds a harmonious and win-win concept of development, provides opportunities for the world through self-development, and takes on international responsibilities matched with its national strength so as to establish a good national image.

The reform and opening-up policy initiates the historical process of China's great changing and reintegrating into the world. For over 30 years, China has experienced more thorough changes than it had in the past 100. The international community is going through a transformation process from looking down upon to treating equally and possibly to looking up at China, a latecomer to the modern international system. At first, the international community, especially the Western countries, regarded China as a target to be transformed, and they tried to influence China's policy through admitting China into the existing international system. In this way, China would become a typical member of the Western bloc. With China's rapid emergence and its persistence in taking an independent approach, however, the West has had to face up to the failure of its transformation strategy. The momentum of China's emergence once again declares the failure of a containment strategy and reshapes the collective mentality of the international community about China. The mentality of the outside world has never been so complex and painful: not only surprised at the miracle of China's development but also anxious about China's future direction; recognizing China's emergence but reluctant to identify with and truly accept the distinctly exotic Chinese way; expecting China to undertake more international responsibilities but full of doubts about China's expanding influence and use of power.

Admittedly, many people of insight hold positive attitudes to China's developmental achievements, realistically analyzing China's development potential and deficiencies and providing important reference for the outside world to have a comprehensive and objective view of China. But for various reasons, most foreigners' perceptions of China are either influenced by prejudice or full of misconceptions. Some of those misconceptions include the following.

The first is the theory of salvation.[1] When the world was plagued by the international financial crisis and the world economy remained gloomy, China not only took the lead in emerging from the crisis and realizing an 8 percent GDP growth rate through the adoption of powerful stimulus policies but also contributed to half of the world's economic growth, becoming an important force for the end of the crisis and the global economic resurgence. Many Westerners reflect upon this phenomenon and wonder how a latecomer to the modern international system can break the declining tendency of the past 100 years, maintain a rapid economic growth for over 30 years in a row, and become the world's second-largest economy. While feeling surprised at China's economic miracle, they began to preach an absurd theory that China is saving the world. In their eyes, China is no longer dispensable in global economic activities and it is not a surprise even to elevate China to the equivalent of the United States as a member of G-2. China's growing GDP and huge foreign exchange reserve are of decisive significance to world economic recovery, and some believe only China can save the capitalist system. Therefore, China is not only capable but also responsible for making a contribution to global well-being.

A second misconception is the China Threat theory,[2] which emerged in the mid and late 1990s and then became increasingly popular along with China's rapid development. It once became a keynote of mainstream international public opinions about China. In the eyes of the proponents of the China threat theory, China is not only incompatible with the mainstream international community but also poses a great challenge in terms of its political regime and strategic security as well as its economic development and ideology. Applying the theory to the development issue, they hold that China's economic freedom and the growth of the middle class do not automatically lead to the arrival of democracy, and political authoritarianism and poor human rights pose a threat to the global democracies. Proponents of the theory also blame China for:

- Gaining competitive advantages through manipulation of exchange rate and reduction of costs, and for aggravating global trade imbalances
- Taking away job opportunities in other countries so that factories remain bankrupt and unemployment continues to increase
- The country's economic growth demanding endless world resources, which directly contributes to the rising prices of primary products in the world

- Explicit "new colonialism" in Africa by investments and development that directly cause the exhaustion of local resources and escalation of conflicts
- Accelerated global warming and environmental deterioration

Proponents hold that because China is the origin of the development problems, they must establish a "united front" to exert pressure on China on various development issues, so as to limit China's development.

The third misconceived theory is that of the free ride.[3] Simply put, this theory holds that since introduction of the reform and opening-up policy, China has achieved great success only because it has benefited from the existing international system and should therefore pay the corresponding costs. If there is no global open and free trade environment and a complete system of division of labor, the vitality of China's economy can hardly be brought into full play and China's development achievements would be greatly abated. China has enjoyed the benefits of the current international order, but some critics say China has refused to share the costs and must now play a more important role as the world's second-largest economy. Further, others say China has shown no willingness to provide public goods for the world, still refusing to pay any costs as a developing country, despite all of its efforts. It is argued that to prevent China from becoming a free rider, it is imperative to establish a new access standard for the international system and to fight back diametrically against China's tough stance in order to regulate China's international behaviors.

Such arguments show that with its growing power, China faces an increasingly complex international public opinion environment. The arguments are partly rational—to a certain extent reflecting the expectations and concerns of the international community about China's future development—yet more of the arguments reflect misunderstanding and confusion about China from the outside world. Clearly, China should not simply reject these arguments in suspicion of conspiracies. Instead, China needs to analyze the formation mechanism of these opinions with great care, settle problems with facts, and convince others by reasoning. Through careful examination, it has been found that there are two basic paths for the emergence of these voices.

First, the publicity for China's image lags behind the specific policy practice. China often does much but speaks little. Even when it does speak, China is accustomed to showing its own image through slogans or abstract language, both of which are difficult to be understood and relatively one-sided. The international community can interpret China only according to its own understanding or even rumors under the context of asymmetric information. Second, what is more important is the serious egocentrism in the international community, especially in the West. China and the West are actually in different stages of the modernization process and therefore have different issues of concern.

China is still in the modernization process, so its priority involves material interests, whereas to a large extent the West is a postmodern society, with human rights, the environment, and other abstract rights as its primary concerns. Convinced that their own claims are of a higher moral value, some Western countries would, without any thinking, judge China's international behavior by their own nations' standards. They actively encourage and advocate whatever is consistent with their desire, thus building unrealistic fantasies and expecting China to make greater "contributions." But when China emphasizes its own particular characteristics, they become angry and rebuke China for its "irresponsible" behaviors, leaving China stranded in a dilemma of morality and interests.

Sometimes there is interaction between these two paths, and that strengthens the respective stable views previously formed. Because China believes that the international community can be full of hostility and malicious intentions, it is hard for China to be completely transparent in stating its policies. Accordingly, the international community can interpret China only according to its own inadequate knowledge of China, further confirming previous bias. Consequently, the perception gap between China and the rest of the world keeps widening, strategic suspicion keeps intensifying, disputes of interests easily become politicized, and the potential costs of interaction keep increasing. If one further considers the changes in the balance of power between

China and other countries caused by the accelerating rise of China, this perception gap would bring about more unpredictable and uncontrollable consequences.

Both China and other countries need an adaptation process to construct a more rational and realistic strategic framework. On one hand, there is a sense of inveterate egocentrism and moral superiority among some foreign countries, which must abate. Reflecting upon the limitation of the modern paradigm based on Western experience when applied to an understanding of China, and truly considering the extraordinary complexities of contemporary China, the ambition and fantasy of transforming China into a typical member of the Western bloc must be given up. On the other hand, China needs to dispel the pessimism of its tortuous history over the past century as well as any impractical and arrogant nationalism in order to foster a healthy and rational national mentality and international understanding, demonstrating the self-confidence of a great power and responding positively to external suspicion while also staying alert against excessively high expectations from abroad so as to demonstrate an objective and diversified image of China to the world.

China and the G-2

Maybe even Fred Bergsten himself could not imagine that the word G-2 that he invented would cause such heated reactions and debates.[4] The concept, which originally referred to Sino-U.S. economic dependence, has become a hot topic in the international community. From the Pacific to the Atlantic, from Moscow to Tokyo, the whole world is discussing the possibility of future China-U.S. cogovernance. Similar to G-2, there is the word *Chimerica*, put forward by Harvard Business School professor Niall Ferguson. In his view, China and the United States have entered a "symbiotic era" and should cooperate with each other, with the United States being the world's largest consumer and China the largest saver. The United States is responsible for the consumption and China is responsible for the production.[5] This also reflects the strong soft power of the United States: for a strategic need, the United States can produce many new concepts for the outside world to consume. Countries in the world act as free propagandists for U.S. interests when they deep process these new words. With the advantage in the international discourse, not only can the United States dominate the agenda setting of the world, but it can even also shape others' values.

To be objective, the popularity of G-2 is not groundless; there are at least three reasons. First, after over three decades of reform and opening up, China has experienced economic growth and accumulation of power. From the Beijing Olympic Games to the National Day parade and to the Shanghai World Expo, China's national capabilities have reached a higher level. In fact, based on its ultralarge geographical size, its huge population, and its broad impact, China has the potential to become a "versatile champion." The international financial crisis has pushed China one step closer to the center of the international arena, making China the focus of the world. Faced with China's emergence, the world is confronted with the need to readjust strategies and policies toward China. From the perspective of China, it can be said that G-2 is the world's new strategic concept, proposed against the context of major changes and adjustments in the international pattern.

Second, the strategic situation of the United States is much different today than it was in the earlier 2000s, when George W. Bush held the office of U.S. president. Foreign strategic blunders and internal economic difficulties during his presidency have resulted in a serious overdraft of U.S. power. Then Barack Obama came into office raising the banner of change and made extensive adjustments in domestic and foreign policies. The important adjustment of his foreign strategy is to outsource responsibilities, which relies on "smart-power diplomacy" and "multipartnership," and China is undoubtedly the most important target of that strategy.[6] The United States hopes to overstate China's international position in exchange for China's strategic support. G-2 is thus put forward as a matter of course.

Third, China and the United States are the world's first- and second-largest economies, so China-U.S. cooperation is indeed essential to healthy and stable development of the world economy. On March 6, 2009, World Bank president Robert Zoellick and Vice President Justin Yifu Lin jointly issued an article—"Recovery Rides on the 'G2'"—in the *Washington Post*, pointing out that for the world's economy to recover, China and the United States, those two economic powerhouses, must cooperate and become the engine for the Group of 20.[7] In an economic sense, G-2 is not unreasonable, but once raised as a leadership structure for China-U.S. cogovernance, it could be politically dangerous and practically infeasible.

In fact, the governments and academia in both China and the United States have tried to avoid using the concept of G-2. Once the concept of G-2 appeared, it was first opposed in the United States. *Foreign Affairs* published an article entitled "The G2 Mirage" enunciating that acknowledgment of China's importance would not cover the discord in the two sides' interests, values, and capabilities. Although the United States needs to cooperate with China to address global challenges, to further upgrade the bilateral relation without addressing the real differences between the two countries would yield no results, leading to mutual blame instead of a successful partnership.[8] Thus, a real G-2 structure would not only weaken the existing superpower status of the United States but also lead to estrangement of the United States and its allies.

Morton Abramowitz, former U.S. assistant secretary of state, said outspokenly that the G-2 arrangement would be unfortunate and that its effective creation would be an extraordinary blow to Japan, America's major ally.[9] This is equally probable for the European Union (EU). Once G-2 is formed, the EU's international role will be more or less marginalized. Therefore, European countries have expressed extensive concern and opposition. Moreover, many people in the United States are against an excessively close China-U.S. relationship because maintaining proper tension in China-U.S. relations serves their interests.

The Chinese people have a more rational and vigilant reaction to the concept of G-2. First, Premier Wen Jiabao said on many occasions that the "pattern of China-U.S. cogovernance" is false and baseless. Chinese academia also holds a negative view, believing that a new concept cannot change the nature of international relations and is not conducive to the healthy development of China-U.S. relations. The media respond with observations like "be G-2-ed" and "do not be misled by G-2." The reason for such a consistent reaction from all circles is first the huge gap between the objective strengths of China and the United States, let alone the gap in scientific and technological strength, military level, and soft power. Even in terms of the most noticeable economic size, China is still far behind the United States. Keeping up appearances and catching up and surpassing through leaping forward are not China's policy options. Therefore the policy makers are clearly aware of China's position, emphasizing China's status as a developing power. China has neither the capacity nor the will to assume global responsibilities equally with the United States.

Second, G-2 is unacceptable both politically and strategically. Politically, "China-U.S. cogovernance" does not conform to the independent foreign policy China has consistently adhered to; it does not conform to China's will to develop friendly cooperation with all countries and seek mutual benefit and win-win; it is against China's established policy of sticking to peaceful development and never seeking hegemony; and it is against China's consistent proposition of all countries participating in the establishment of a harmonious multipolar world.[10] Strategically, once China accepts the notion of G-2, China would be the focus of conflicting interests in the world, thereby increasing frictions with the European Union, Japan, and other traditional powers; causing jealousy from other emerging powers; raising doubts among neighboring countries; and alienating other developing countries.

Third, the nature of world politics is undergoing significant changes: globalization has accelerated the diffusion of international power, causing more cross-border issues; however, the democratization trend requires all stakeholders to solve problems through equal consultations; and the collective emergence of developing countries means that multipolarization would be the general trend. Future international structure will be the coexistence of multipowers instead of China-U.S. cogovernance. Therefore, both the world trend and

China's actual power and political realities leave no room for the concept of G-2.

Just like other buzzwords, G-2 has gradually faded out of people's vision due to recent frictions and battles on a series of issues between China and the United States. Pessimistic views on China-U.S. relations once again become the dominant international public opinion. This shows that as China's strength increases and its policies and behaviors change, the outside world's perception of China is also in dynamic adjustment. It also suggests that when dealing with relations with foreign countries, we need to have a rational view of the cooperation and differences between both sides. We should never have unrealistic expectations because of a harmonious relationship. Nor should we regard normal interest disputes as political principles or matters of good and evil. As for the positioning of China raised by G-2, it seems more appropriate to define China as a relatively strong regional power with rising status in a group of emerging countries.

Shoulder the Responsibility of Poverty Alleviation

Poverty is a world problem since ancient times and still plagues modern society. Billions of people all over the world are still desperately struggling in poverty. They cannot enjoy basic living security, medical care, or education. They have no extravagant hopes for, and have never even heard of, the modern standard of living. According to statistics, there are still over a billion absolutely poor people in the world living on less than US$1 a day; about 800 million live in food insecurity or cannot work normally or live healthily due to hunger.[10b]

Of course, the international community has made sustained efforts to alleviate poverty. In September 2000, the UN held a summit meeting and confirmed Millennium Development Goals to alleviate global poverty by the Millennium Declaration, with the goal of halving the poor population in the world by 2015 and requiring countries to make great improvements in education, gender equality, health care, poverty elimination, and environment protection. Political leaders, entrepreneurs, and entertainment celebrities all make important contributions to world poverty reduction. However, worldwide poverty remains grave to date. UN secretary-general Ban Ki-moon said in Millennium Development Goals Report 2010 that "improvements in the lives of the poor have been unacceptably slow, and some hard-won gains are being eroded by the climate, food and economic crises."[11] In the State of Food Insecurity in the World 2009, the Food and Agriculture Organization of the United Nations estimated that 1.02 billion people were undernourished worldwide in 2009, up by 11 percent compared with 2008, due to the financial crisis and rising food prices and other factors. The current world population is about 6.7 billion, meaning that about one-sixth of the world's population are suffering from hunger, and almost all of those hungry people are in developing countries. Among them, most of the hungry live in Asia and the Pacific region: about 642 million; 265 million are in sub-Saharan Africa; 53 million are in Latin America and the Caribbean; 42 million are the Middle East and North Africa; 15 million are in developed countries. In addition, the proportion of hungry people in sub-Saharan Africa is the highest, about 32 percent.[12] Undoubtedly, the prospect of global poverty alleviation is unpromising, and there is still a long way to go to achieve the Millennium Development Goals.

China has undoubtedly made the most significant achievement in poverty reduction in the world. Since introduction of the reform and opening-up policy, the Chinese government, from the strategic perspective of guaranteeing all people the rights to subsistence and development, has adhered to the idea and policy of development-oriented poverty relief and actively encouraged and mobilized social forces to participate so that the population in absolute poverty has become greatly reduced in a short period of time. According to the Chinese government's poverty standard, the number of poverty-stricken people in rural China with problems obtaining sufficient food and clothing decreased from 250 million in 1978 to 14.79 million in 2007; and the impoverishment rate there decreased from 30.7 percent to 1.6 percent. The number of people with adequate food and clothing but unstable and low income decreased from 62.13 million in 2000 to 28.41 million in 2007, constituting 6.7 percent of the total rural population in

2000 and 3 percent in 2007.[13] This means that among all the people who have gotten out of poverty in the world, over 90 percent are in China. China has achieved the United Nations Millennium Development Goal of halving the proportion of the poor population ahead of schedule, laying a solid foundation for the realization of the Millennium Goals. In addition, China has made gratifying achievements in promoting basic education, sanitation improvements, AIDS prevention and control, and nutrition improvements for infants and young children, greatly improving the Chinese people's average life span and health level.

At the same time, China is also an active participant in global poverty reduction. As China's overall economic strength rises, China has gradually increased its efforts to offer aid to poor countries, relieved or exempted the debts of some poor countries, and provided various economic and technical support. In 2005, the Chinese government, the United Nations Development Programme, and other international organizations jointly set up the International Poverty Reduction Center in China and made it a platform for actively holding international poverty reduction training, communication, and research. The center has trained 191 middle- or high-ranking officials from 58 countries, organized seven international conferences on poverty reduction, and invited officials, practitioners, and researchers from nearly 100 countries and international organizations to come to China for exchanges, studies, and inspections. In addition, the Chinese government has made donations to the African Development Fund, the Asian Development Fund, and other agencies and has set up an Asian Development Bank fund for poverty reduction and regional cooperation. All these efforts reflect China's support for world and regional development, with significant contributions to promoting poverty reduction cooperation and exchanges of experience in the developing world.

Poverty eradication is the biggest development issue. The international community has the responsibility of ensuring the basic rights of food and subsistence for hungry people. Undeniably, China still faces a tough poverty reduction mission not only based on its large absolute number of poor people, low levels of education, regional variations, and other major problems but also influenced by natural disasters, economic crises, and other uncertain factors. But generally speaking, China's economic development and poverty reduction measures have lifted the vast majority of Chinese out of desperate poverty and guaranteed them a basic well-off life. With its huge population, China has made an outstanding contribution to improving overall human living conditions and welfare. China's poverty reduction achievements are of global significance. On the other hand, without great success in China, the world's poverty reduction report card would be not worth mentioning. Just as the United Nations assistant secretary-general said, China is a leading force in promoting the Millennium Development Goals; it had made crucial contributions for the UN Millennium Development goals to be achieved before 2015 on schedule.[14] China's efforts to help other developing countries in the world to alleviate poverty within its power also show China's assumption of international responsibilities. In order to achieve the fundamental ideal of human freedom from want, China will continue to make efforts for global poverty reduction together with the international community.

China and Africa Relations

Africa has suffered from great adversities and humiliation since it became passively involved in the modern world, and it is still plagued by poverty, hunger, infectious diseases, ethnic conflicts, and years of civil wars even today. Problems left over by history, weak political and social systems, and unfair international orders beset African countries' modernization attempts with difficulties. After the end of the Cold War, negative effects of globalization emerged; changes in the international pattern led to a power vacuum; and many countries had difficulties in their modernization process. Under such circumstances, African countries are in an exacerbated governance plight, with many even reduced to the ranks of failed states. But the African people are also getting united and making significant progress in regional cooperation and economic development. In addition, the international community is making investments in and offering aid to Africa. The dawn of revival is breaking upon Africa in the new century.

Both China and Africa have experienced the historical process of colonial rule and national liberation. As developing regions, both China and African countries have a strong demand for speeding up modernization and achieving national prosperity and are committed to changing the unjust international political and economic order and achieving global justice. Since the 1950s and 1960s, China has carried forward the spirit of internationalism, offering selfless assistance to the anti-imperialist movements in Africa and economic and social development and establishing a deep friendship between China and Africa. Since introduction of the reform and opening-up policy, with its economic development and growing national strength, China has made greater efforts to offer aid to Africa, helping Africa alleviate poverty and achieve development. China-Africa economic and trade cooperation has shown a momentum of rapid development: the growth rate in bilateral trade volume had been over 30 percent for eight years since exceeding US$10 billion in 2000 and exceeding US$100 billion in 2008, reaching US$106.8 billion.[15] Meanwhile, China and Africa have had all-around cooperation in political dialogues, cultural exchanges, and other fields, achieving mutual benefit and win-win strategies and setting a perfect example of South-South cooperation.

However, China's trade with Africa and its investments in Africa have triggered some Westerners' envy and complaints. There is concern that China's presence would lead to a loss of their advantages and a drop in their benefits. The title "new colonialism," which was originally used to criticize the West for extracting excessive profits and depriving the former colonies of their rights to development is now imposed upon China.[16] In their view, Africa has been reduced to a colony for China to dump goods and plunder resources: plenty of cheap made-in-China goods have destroyed local enterprises in Africa, causing a growing number of the population to be unemployed; under-the-table deals exist in oil development, without any consideration for local ecological environment and welfare; and disregard for human rights situations results in aid flowing into the pockets of dictators, thereby brewing corruption and conflicts. Former British foreign secretary Jack Straw even listed China as one of the top 10 challenges faced by Africa, along with poverty, regional conflicts, and terrorism.[17] In short, they claim that what China is doing in Africa now is much the same as what the West did 150 years ago.

China should not laugh off these groundless accusations but needs to criticize and refute them with reason and restraint. In fact, most of the problems in Africa today are legacies of the colonial era, when a large number of Africans were trafficked, the land was divided up, and resources were plundered. All these have left Africa with birth defects in economic and social development. After the Western colonial powers were forced to withdraw, Africa had only a superstructure and was in extreme poverty.

In contrast to the criticisms from the Western media, China's activities in Africa have offered a rare opportunity for the local economy. China-Africa economic and trade cooperation is carried out based on the premise of equality and mutual benefit. China's import of resources and raw materials from Africa has improved the local economic conditions and relatively single trade channel, increasing the independence of African exports. While investing in Africa, China adheres to the unity of economic and social benefits, focusing on local infrastructure construction and ecological environment protection and safeguarding the sustainability of local economic development. China has offered as much help as possible to Africa to improve the capacity of local independent development, including debt relief, construction projects, technical support, and personnel training.

At the China-Africa summit of November 2006, the Chinese government put forward a policy package of eight measures to extend aid to Africa.[18] In 2009, at the Fourth Ministerial Conference of Forum on China-Africa Cooperation, Premier Wen Jiabao announced eight new measures to promote China-Africa cooperation.[19] In order to expand imports from African countries, the Chinese government since 2005 has in succession granted the exemption of customs duty for 478 tax items imported into China from 31 least-developed countries in Africa (according to 2009 China Customs Tariff Schedule 8-digit code based on the Harmonized System). By the end of November 2009, favored commodities imported from Africa into China had totaled US$1.03 billion. Favored commodities include sesame, unwrought refined copper, cobalt, and goatskin.[20] In addition, by the end of October 2009, China had provided preferential loans for 28 African countries, supporting 53 projects, and providing preferential export buyer's credit for 11 projects.

Construction of the African Union Conference Center was started in December 2008 and was completed on January 29, 2012. Cancellation of the interest-free loan debt due at the end of 2005 from heavily indebted poor countries and least-developed countries in Africa has been basically completed. China has also expanded the range of zero-tariff favored commodities imported from the least-developed countries in Africa, and has trained 14,000 personnel for Africa, and has sent out 104 agricultural experts and 281 young volunteers to Africa.[21]

What China has done for Africa has nothing to do with neo-colonialism. On the contrary, it has brought tangible benefits to African economic development. According to an article in the German magazine *Wirtschafts Woche*, China "contributed to an increase of more than 5 percent of the African economy and the lowest inflation rate in 25 years. And it was the first time in African history that capital in form of investments surpassed capital in form of aid. Although like what the European colonists had done in history, China also built roads and railways to the mine resources in Angola. They built their roads and railways through where the farmers, businesspeople, and craftsmen live so that they could go to the nearby markets to sell their goods and provide services. It is not China's obligation to supervise whether African countries are using this historic opportunity to integrate into globalization. It is the first time in history that the Africans can command their own fate—a rare opportunity created by the Chinese."[22]

Africa is in a strategic position in China's overall diplomatic layout. Its importance will further increase with the expansion of China's national interests. Other powers are also formulating overall strategies toward Africa, increasing investments of resources in Africa.

China should strengthen communication and enhance understanding between itself and the West in regard to its actions in, and support of, Africa in order to reduce misunderstanding and tension caused by lack of understanding. China will continue to strengthen China-Africa mutually beneficial cooperation with a responsible attitude, giving more benefits to Africans and helping them achieve development.

Great Success Achieved in Foreign Aid

Foreign aid is an important part of the international relations and diplomatic strategy of a country. As the most important socialist country and developing country in the world, China has always regarded foreign aid as the fulfillment of international obligations and an important measure to promote the establishment of a new international order and a harmonious world. The year 2010 was the sixtieth anniversary of China's foreign aid. For those 60 years, China persisted in providing economic and technological aid for developing countries while it committed to its own development, in improving economic and social conditions in the recipient countries, in enhancing their capacities for independent development, and in making an outstanding contribution to peace and development in the cause of humankind. Meanwhile, China has deepened its friendly and cooperative relations with the recipient countries, adding new glory to harmonious win-win relations and eternal friendships in the developing world.

Since the founding of the People's Republic of China, foreign aid has always been a basic component of China's foreign policy. It also reflects an important aspect of the evolution of relations with other countries. However, with changes in national power and shifts in strategic focus, the target countries, content, and methods of China's foreign aid have undergone changes in different stages. In the early days of the People's Republic of China, China began foreign aid when its own economy was underdeveloped. Influenced by the principles of socialism and anti-imperialism and the anticolonialism movements in the world, China's distribution of foreign aid was carried out as a "serious political activity," mainly targeting socialist countries and emerging national independent countries. In 1964, when Premier Chou En-lai was on a visit to 11 African countries, he put forward the famous eight principles of foreign aid that became an important guiding doctrine of China's foreign aid to developing countries.[23] China's foreign economic aid accounted for 4.5 percent of the country's financial expenditure in 1967, and in 1972 increased to 6.7 percent, totaling more than 5.1 billion RMB. In 1973 it rose to 7.2 percent, surpassing the world's most developed and richest countries.[24] By 1976, China had provided economic aid for more than 110 countries and regions, including the DPRK, Vietnam, and Albania. It is clear that before reform and opening up, the target and form of China's foreign aid were relatively simple, but the amount was huge—even beyond the actual capacity of China's national economy.

After the implementation of reform and opening up, China made some adjustments in its foreign aid policy, highlighting "equality and mutual benefit, diverse forms, emphasis on effects and common development."[25] First, economic considerations outweighed political and ideological pursuits. Thus, foreign aid began to develop in an equal, mutually beneficial, healthy, and sustainable direction. On one hand, foreign aid promoted economic development and social progress in the recipient countries; on the other hand, foreign aid enhanced economic and technological cooperation between China and the recipient countries, thus achieving the goal of common development and prosperity.

Second, the single-sided form of aid was changed. In addition to loans and free assistance, China cooperated with the recipient countries in technical guidance, personnel training, medical assistance, education, humanitarian relief, and other aspects. Third, China gradually made more efforts in extending foreign aid with the increase in its national strength while insisting on the priority of domestic development. During this period, China still adhered to the principle of non-interference in internal affairs with foreign aid. In the face of internal conflicts of the recipient countries, China advocated seeking solutions through political dialogues. Meanwhile, China mainly provided aid directly to the recipient countries, with relatively inactive participation in multilateral international cooperation and policy coordination.

Generally speaking, the adjustment in foreign aid policy helped achieve mutual benefit and win-win between China and the recipient countries. But China's "unconditional" and "acting-alone" approach was questioned by the international community.

With China's accelerated emergence and the establishment of responsible power strategy, China has become more rational and more mature in its distribution of foreign aid. First, China seeks a balance between the principle of non-interference and humanitarian considerations. Just as Professor Zhou Qi of the Institute of American Studies at the Chinese Academy of Social Sciences says, "The century-long humiliation that China underwent in modern history made the Western imperialists' deeds including invasion and intervention remain fresh in the country's memory; as a result, it pays more heed to the diplomatic principles of respecting sovereignty. But if China wants to show the world it is a responsible nation, it must well balance the principle of insisting on not interfering in others' internal affairs and the will to boost resolving the humanitarian crises in the international community."[26] In fact, China has gradually changed its previous approaches—for instance, by shouldering corresponding humanitarian responsibilities in facilitating solution of the Darfur issue in Sudan.

Second, China has actively pursued a balance between its unilateral assistance and international multilateral cooperation. In 1997, China began to actively participate in multilateral aid to international organizations. In 2000, China provided multilateral aid for the World Food Programme, the United Nations Development Programme, and 10 other international organizations. In addition, China has substantially increased its contributions to the United Nations and has joined the list of donor countries of the World Bank International Development Association. All these show that China's concept of foreign aid is undergoing important changes, with more emphasis on coordination and cooperation with the international community.

Third, China carefully keeps a balance between national capacity and international responsibilities. Deviating from current national conditions and assuming too much responsibility would cause an overdraft of China's own capacity, but insufficient foreign aid would not comply with China's image of a responsible power. Therefore, China attaches great importance to acting according to its capability and striving for the best.

In retrospect, China has achieved great success in foreign aid in the past 60 years. Since 1950, China has provided aid for more than 160 countries in Asia, Africa, eastern Europe, Latin America, and South Pacific regions, helping the recipient countries complete nearly 2,000 projects closely related to the local peoples. About 100,000 officials and managerial and technical personnel have come to attend trainings and studies in China. China has provided government scholarships for more than 70,000 international students from developing countries. China has repeatedly offered immediate humanitarian assistance to countries suffering from major natural disasters. In the past five years, the Chinese government has carried out nearly 200 foreign emergency relief operations.[26b] Since 2000, China has waived the interest due on loans to heavily indebted poor countries and least-developed countries. Up to now, China has signed debt exemption protocols with 50 countries, exempting 380 due debts.[27] All of these demonstrate China's concerns over development issues and its assumption of international responsibilities. China is growing into a responsible power with an active attitude.

Promoting the Development of Human Rights

The issue of human rights in China has been greatly criticized internationally, specifically by Western countries, and China has often passively responded with occasional retorts. In fact, since the founding of the People's Republic of China, especially since introduction of the reform and opening-up policy, China has made unprecedented progress in the development of human rights. The human rights situation in the closed and backward past period cannot be compared to that in the People's Republic of China. The Chinese government regards "respecting and safeguarding human rights" as an important principle of governance and writes it in the Constitution, takes "people-oriented" as the basic concept of ruling, and adopts various measures to improve the material and cultural levels of the entire population; and it conscientiously protects people's political, economic, and cultural rights, thus laying a solid foundation for comprehensive development of the Chinese people and for making a great contribution to promotion of human rights in the world.

In today's world, human rights has become a major issue of common concern in the international community. To achieve full human rights is a long-sought ideal of mankind and also a long-term goal of China. However, it should be noted that countries differ considerably in their historical backgrounds, cultural traditions, economic development conditions, and other aspects, which fundamentally determines that each country's approaches and processes of achieving the ideal of human rights will differ. In the historical evolution of the development of human rights, countries should promote human rights according to their own circumstances and real conditions. The Chinese government not only respects the principle of the universality of human rights but also addresses human rights issues based on its national conditions.[28] Meanwhile, despite the international aspect of the human rights issue, it is mainly a problem within the scope of a sovereign state. Arguments such as "human rights over sovereignty" in the international community are prone to interfere grossly in countries' sovereignty and are not conducive to the overall development of international human rights.

The Chinese government has formed its own views on human rights based on China's history and national conditions and has formulated corresponding laws and policies promoting the development of human rights through concrete actions and unremitting efforts. With regard to the priority of human rights, China has always put the right to subsistence and development first and regarded it as the foundation of the realization of other economic, political, and cultural rights. That is to say, for a developing country like China, safeguarding and realizing subsistence and development remain the primary tasks of promoting human rights. Since the founding of the People's Republic of China, the Chinese people's material living standard has realized a historical leap from insufficient food and clothing to moderate prosperity. In more than 60 years since the founding of the People's

Republic of China, especially since introduction of the reform and opening-up policy, China's economic growth rate has been among the highest in the world.

By 2008, China's per-capita GDP had increased from 119 RMB in 1952 to 22,698 RMB; deducting price factors, increased by 32.4 times, with an average annual growth rate of 6.5 percent per capita; gross income had reached US$3.292 million, raising China to the ranks of middle-income countries of the world, according to the criteria of World Bank.[29] China has solved the problem of feeding 22 percent of the world's people with only 9 percent of the world's arable land, people's average life expectancy has significantly increased, the illiteracy rate has steeply reduced, nine-year compulsory education is widely available, and the social security system is constantly improved. There is no doubt that these are historic achievements China has made in protecting human rights.

Certainly, China's human rights consist not just of rights to subsistence but also of political, economic, cultural, and social rights. Since 1978, the democratization of China's political life has developed continuously: systems of democratic election, democratic policy making, democratic management, and democratic supervision have improved; democratic politics have been institutionalized and standardized and have due procedures; ordered political participation of citizens has expanded; and people's rights to information, participation, expression, and supervision are effectively protected along the track of institutionalization. China has formulated 229 laws in force, more than 600 administrative regulations in force, and over 7,000 local laws and regulations in force, forming a fairly complete legal system with the Constitution as the core. China basically has laws to go by in economy, politics, culture, and other aspects of social life. And citizens' rights and freedoms can be fully respected and protected in the legislative, executive, and judicial sectors.[30]

China recognizes and respects the purposes and principles of protecting and promoting human rights in the Charter of the United Nations, appreciates and supports the efforts made by the United Nations to universally promote human rights, and actively participates in the activities of the United Nations in the human rights field. China highly values the important role of international human rights instruments in promoting and protecting human rights. Up to now, China has acceded to 25 international human rights treaties and actively fulfills the treaty obligations. Through constructive dialogues with the treaty bodies, as well as consideration of its national conditions, China adopts and implements their reasonable and practicable suggestions. The United Nations Human Rights Council (UNHRC) established in 2006 is the specialized agency of the United Nations that deals with human rights affairs. China was elected as a member of the UNHRC in 2006 and 2009, making an important contribution to the UNHRC and making unremitting efforts to achieve the lofty goal of promoting and protecting human rights.

Since the 1990s, under the support of many developing countries, China has thwarted some Western countries' attempts to make anti-China motions in the UNHRC 11 times, thereby defending national sovereignty and national dignity. China has published eight white papers introducing the overall situation of human rights in China, more than 30 special white papers, and a number of important articles on the human rights issue, comprehensively and systematically introducing to foreign countries China's basic situation, policies, and views of the human rights issue. In response to foreign countries' concern over the human rights issue in China, China has timely and officially clarified the facts, expressed its policy and position, refuted distorted accusations by international hostile forces, removed misunderstanding from abroad, and won wide understanding and support in the international community.[31] At the same time, the Chinese government is committed to developing exchanges and cooperation in international human rights based on equality and mutual respect by promoting the healthy development of international human rights causes. China has established human rights dialogue mechanisms with Western countries and regions such as the United States, Japan, Germany, Britain, the EU, and Australia. By June 2010, China had conducted 29 human rights dialogues with the EU and 15 human rights dialogues with the United States.

The Chinese government unswervingly pushes forward the cause of human rights in China and in response to the United Nations' call for establishing a national human rights action plan, instituted the National Human Rights Action Plan of China (2009–2010) on April 13, 2009, on the basis of a full summary of past experience and an objective analysis of the current situation.[32] The document explains the policy of the Chinese government with regard to the promotion and protection of human rights during the period 2009–2010, covering political, economic, social, and cultural fields. This was an important event in the history of China's human rights development. It has become a key theme of China's national construction and social development, marking a new stage of planned and comprehensive promotion for China's human rights development. The plan defines the Chinese government's goals in promoting and protecting human rights and the specific measures it would take to this end in the coming two years. It was also another major effort made by the Chinese government to promote the development of human rights.

Case Study—Medical Rescue Abroad and Responsibilities of China

"With sorrows of separation from the family and holy prides of devotion to Benin, and not knowing the date of return, I tearfully said goodbye to my children and parents and set foot for the first time on the expedition to West Africa, going on the sacred mission of my country." This is in the diary written by Zou Guangzhen in 1978, when she was leaving with a medical assistance team for Benin. Over 70 years old, Zou is now an expert on obstetrics and gynecology at the Affiliated Hospital of Ningxia Medical University. Recalling the special medical experience over 30 years ago, Zou is filled with deep feelings. In response to the government's call, Ningxia Hui Autonomous Region organized the first medical assistance team consisting of 23 people. On January 5, 1978, the team went to Benin on behalf of China to perform a medical aid mission, and Zou was one of them. Although the medical staff had psyched themselves up for the hard living conditions there, they were really surprised by the lack of basic wards, medical equipment, and even water and electricity. In the difficult and poverty-stricken working environment, the love and persistent pursuit for medical work and timeless faith in China enabled Zou Guangzhen and other medical team members to be fearless of the hardships and dangers and to vanquish obstacles.[33]

The year 2008 was the thirtieth anniversary of Ningxia's sending medical assistance teams to the Republic of Benin. In those 30 years, Ningxia medical assistance teams made brilliant achievements. Sixteen batches of 364 medical staff devoted their prime years to the national foreign aid cause, among whom Wang Shula, Liu Yurong, and Li Shufeng sacrificed their lives. According to incomplete statistics, Ningxia medical assistance teams in Benin provided diagnosis and treatment for 2 million people who had various types of common diseases and frequently occurring diseases; the teams performed 47,000 operations; and they actively created conditions to conduct complicated surgeries that rescued critically ill patients.[34] In those 30 years, the medical teams successfully performed cardiac injury surgery, cerebral surgery, lobectomy of liver, radical operation of mastocarcinoma, large-tumor resection, intraocular lens transplantation, and large-area allogeneic skin graft.[35] Meanwhile, the Ningxia medical teams trained medical staff in Benin and gave lectures on epidural anesthesia, child toxic dysentery, normal childbirth, diagnosis and treatment of anemia, liver function test, fluoroscopy of chest, and aseptic technique. The teams also wrote a book titled *African Child Cerebral Malaria—100 Cases of Prevention and Treatment* and left the book for Benin doctors, thereby bequeathing an "ever-present medical assistance team" for the local people.[36] It is that medical staff's hard work and selfless dedication that saved a lot of lives and created one miracle after another, adding touching glory to the eternal friendship between China and Benin.

Benin is only one of the target countries to which China has sent medical aid in the past 50 years. Since 1963, when China sent out the first medical aid team to Algeria, China's foreign medical teams have spread to every corner of the world. By 2008, China had sent foreign medical teams to 69 countries and regions in Asia, Africa, Latin America, Europe, and Oceania—medical staff totaling 20,679—and the number of patients in the recipient countries who received treatment from Chinese doctors had reached 260 million. Currently, there are still 50 Chinese foreign medical teams in 48 countries on five continents: 1,278 medical staff working in 123 medical institutions and providing free medical services. Provinces, autonomous regions, and cities across the country bear the task of sending out foreign medical teams.[37]

The medical assistance staff bear in mind the great trust of the party and the nation, go forth with an international humanitarian spirit, and work creatively in poorly equipped and drug-lacking environments, thus making an outstanding contribution to promoting health care and people's health in the recipient countries and receiving a warm welcome and wide praise from the government and peoples of the recipient countries. In 40 years, nearly 900 medical team members have received honors from leaders of the recipient countries. Chinese medical teams are called the "white angels" and the "most welcome people." With regard to the duration, scale, number of recipient countries, and effect of foreign medical aid, the remarkable achievements made by China's foreign medical assistance cannot be compared with any other country in the world and are truly rare in the history of international relations.

In more than 40 years, China's foreign medical aid teams have cured large numbers of patients in the recipient countries, bringing great changes to local peoples. Moreover, the teams also practiced their superb skills with realistic and innovative spirit and filled many blanks in the recipient countries' medical histories. In July 1985, a Chinese medical team in Tripoli, Libya, successfully conducted a complete leg replantation. In 1991, another Chinese team in Equatorial Guinea successfully conducted the first craniotomy. A doctor on the Chinese medical team in Taza, Morocco, successfully conducted an operation on a patient with a deformity of the left forearm, filling the dearth of treatment of congenital malformations in the Taza region.[38] Chinese acupuncture in particular has obtained a good reputation in the recipient countries. For instance, among the 57,330 patients cured by the medical team in Niger in 2006, 5,120 were treated with acupuncture. And many government ministers became keenly interested in Chinese medicine and acupuncture.[39] In addition, Chinese medical teams take into consideration the actual needs of the recipient countries and carry out various forms of health assistance, including helping build medical centers, organizing a variety of professional trainings, providing medical technology consultancy, conducting research, and greatly improving levels of health care and treatment capabilities in the recipient countries. As early as 1965, when Premier Chou En-lai visited Zanzibar, he told medical team members: "Chinese medical teams will leave sooner or later. We ought to train the medical staff in Zanzibar so that they can work independently, leaving an ever-present medical team to the local people, for the liberation of African people."[40]

In retrospect, China's foreign medical aid has achieved great success in the past decades. China took the initiative to assume international humanitarian responsibility when it was itself in extreme poverty and had before it the arduous task of development but contributed to improving the overall living standards of other developing countries, thereby demonstrating China's care for the well-being of humankind. As China's national strength continues to grow, the scale and capacity of China's foreign medical teams have been expanding. After several decades of development, foreign medical aid has become an important part of China's diplomacy, deepening the mutually beneficial cooperation between China and other developing countries and establishing a peaceful and friendly international image of China.

CHINA'S GROWTH AND THE INTERNATIONAL ECONOMY

An emerging-market economy is one of China's many identities in today's international community. As China pushes ahead on its way to peaceful development, it actively gets integrated into the current international economic system, takes part in international economic exchange and cooperation with a peaceful and cooperative attitude, and assumes its national responsibilities to advance international economic systems toward just and reasonable directions. At the same time as the policy of opening up, China also places emphasis on its endogenous capacity building and sustainable development to enhance the quality of economic and social development and to promote common prosperity around the world.

In the twenty-first century, the world is undergoing profound changes, and under themes of peace and development, economic globalization and regional economic integration are witnessing rare developments. Economic factors, too, play increasingly important roles in international relations. In the global economic race, China's sustaining and outstanding performance attracts the world's attention and manifests its readiness to take on international responsibilities.

China's strong economic growth has gone hand in hand with its social development. The country's average annual economic growth rate from 1978 to 2008 reached 9.8 percent. The global financial crisis in 2008 exposed many defects in the Western development model, represented by the United States, and demonstrated the necessity of *multiple* development models of different types to learn from each other. The financial crisis seriously affected China's economy as well, resulting in significantly decreasing exports and increasing unemployment rates. Facing these difficulties, the Chinese government implemented fully and improved continuously its package program and other policies dealing with the impact of the international financial crisis and became the first in the world to achieve economic recovery. In 2009, China's gross domestic product reached 33.5 trillion RMB, up by 8.7 percent compared with 2008.

Since 2010, China's economy has maintained steady and relatively fast growth, and annual economic growth is expected to reach over 9 percent. In the first 10 years of the twenty-first century, average annual growth rate of China's economy was more than 10 percent as well. In terms of internal logic, those excellent performances are consistent with the great achievements made in the 30 years of China's reform and opening up. The performances also have roots in the basic principles and spirit of China's handling of domestic and foreign affairs—that is, adhering to the unity of independence and opening up, taking both the domestic and international situations into consideration, absorbing the essence of traditional Chinese culture as well as learning from all of China's achievements, and thinking both carefully and innovatively. China's success draws the attention of the world, which started studying China's unique development model—the "China Model."

On a deeper level, the China Model is the result of mutual promotion between the socialist system with Chinese characteristics and traditional Chinese culture, which is helping China develop quickly from a traditional peasant society into one of the largest industrialized countries in the world, bearing the great responsibilities of progress and development of human society.

China has solved the survival and development problems of about 22 percent of the global population and has therefore ensured long-term prosperity and stability in an important region of East Asia. As President Hu Jintao said in 2008, "We [China] solved the problem of feeding 1.3 billion people on our own. The agricultural and industrial production of our country has ranked the first in the world. Major scientific and technological innovations of the world's advanced level are emerging. The high-tech industries are booming. Water, energy, transportation and communications and other infrastructure have major breakthroughs. Ecological establishment continues to develop. And urban and rural areas have taken on a completely new look."[1]

The steady and rapid economic growth has laid an important foundation for China's development of a well-off and harmonious society and will keep on promoting the Chinese people's comprehensive development. China also provided strong impetus for the global economy and enhanced the well-being of people around the world.

Since introduction of the reform and opening-up policy, China has adopted an attitude of cooperation with the international community, taken a wider and deeper part in international cooperation, and become an important engine of the world economy with its increased contribution to world economic growth. In 2009, China contributed more than 50 percent to global gross domestic product growth, which was the first time that a developing country led the world in economic growth. On June 17, 2010, the result of a global poll conducted by the Pew Research Center of the United States showed that the percentage of people who consider China as the world's leading economy has risen from 20 percent to 31 percent.

China's modernization is fundamentally different from the mode of foreign expansion of early capitalist countries in Europe and America. It recognizes self-reliance as the basic point of development and realizes its sustainable growth through a free market and open cooperation. China's development will not harm the national interests of other countries; on the contrary, it will facilitate mutual benefit and common development.

Around the world, it is not a singular phenomenon that China has achieved rapid and sustained economic development at the beginning of the twenty-first century. There are a large number of emerging-market economies. In 2003, financial services firm Goldman Sachs raised the concept of "BRICs" for the first time, followed by the "Next-11" in 2005, whose growth potentials are just after the BRICs. In 2007, some Japanese experts put forward the five countries of "VISTA."[2] These emerging economies seize the opportunity of economic globalization by accelerating domestic reform and adjustment, by expanding, and by opening up, resulting in tremendous economic and social development as well as rising international status and influence.

During the eight-year period of Vladimir Putin's presidency, Russia's economy maintained rapid growth, with a GDP increase of 72 percent and an average annual growth rate of around 7 percent. Affected by the global financial crisis, the growth rate of Russia's GDP in 2008 decreased to 5.6 percent and its GDP in 2009 dropped by 7.9 percent over the previous year. But in the first half of 2010, the economic recovery showed good momentum. It is estimated that the annual economic growth rate will be 3 percent and that Russia will speed up its way out of the crisis.

India has maintained a fast and sustained economic development since the reform in 1991. The average annual growth rate of GDP was 5.9 percent from 1990 to 2000, 7.4 percent from 2001 to 2006, and 9 percent in 2007. Due to the financial crisis, the growth rate of GDP in fiscal year 2008 dropped to 6.7 percent, which is still much higher than that of the major developed countries in Europe and America. Brazil's economic strength ranks first in South America and eighth in the world. The country's growth rates in GDP in 2007 and 2008 were 5.4 percent and 5.1 percent, respectively. Thanks to proper measures against the crisis, GDP dropped by only 2 percent in 2009. In 2010, the economic growth rate of GDP was 7.5 percent, and in 2011, it was 2.7 percent.

The overall rise of the emerging markets has become a significant phenomenon in the evolution of international relations in the new century. Emerging markets have become (1) the important driving force for the global economy, (2) major suppliers and huge markets, and (3) positive guardians and promoters of global free trade. According to some experts, the rise of the emerging-market economies is the third power transfer in the past 500 years. And such a structural power transfer will establish a new international pattern. However, it is undeniable that these emerging markets still face a lot of difficulties, including economic restructuring and financial market reform. They need to focus on their own long-term and sustainable development and to undertake international responsibilities within their capacity at the same time.

Reform the International
Financial System

The global financial crisis triggered by the subprime crisis in the United States has impacted the global financial market seriously and threatened the stable development of real economy, reflecting the enormous loopholes in the monetary policies and financial regulation and innovations of the United States and leading to further reflection on the current international financial system.

After the breakdown of the Bretton Woods system in the 1970s, the gold and U.S. dollar standard system collapsed and international currencies appeared to be having a trend of diversification, with the status of the euro and the yen going upward. But the U.S. dollar is still the most important reserve currency of the world and the major medium of international financial trade,[3] and it still holds the monopoly and hegemony position in the current international monetary system. So some experts refer to this system as the dollar standard system. In such a financial system, the tremendous and ever-expanding trade deficit, excessive internal consumption, and debts increase the risks of the U.S. economic operation directly. In case of the crisis, other countries were implicated and paid for the huge debts, and the global economy got into turmoil. And emerging economies depending on high export volumes were seriously struck.

The global financial crisis is a profound lesson. With the development of a global economy, the system design and operation by the international financial institutions represented by the International Monetary Fund (IMF) and the World Bank become more and more unsuitable for changes in the international economic and financial structure, and therefore they cannot play full roles in global economic and financial affairs. China sees the distribution of special quota and voting rights as unfair because developing countries lack representation.[4] Although China became the largest holder of foreign exchange reserves, the world's second-largest trading nation, and the third-largest economy and its GDP accounts for 6.4 percent of that of the world, its voting right is only 3.66 percent in the IMF. And lacking a transparent rule, the quota distribution is much inclined to be political and becomes the result of political negotiations and trading between members, especially between the major developed countries.[5] The imbalance of decision-making rights causes international financial institutions to serve the interests of some of the developed countries instead of the basic demands of most people in the world. With their rapid rise, the emerging markets have raised their awareness of participation in the international financial field controlled by a few developed countries, and the voice calling for international economic justice is growing louder.

As the largest emerging economy, China actively supports reform for a fair, just, tolerant, and well-managed international financial system and works toward a new international economic and financial order. On November 15, 2008, at the G-20 Financial Summit, Chinese President Hu Jintao said that those crucial reforms ought to be implemented in a comprehensive, balanced, incremental, and result-oriented manner. "A comprehensive reform is one that has a general design and includes measures to improve not only the international financial system, monetary system and financial institutions, but also international financial rules and procedures. A balanced reform is one that is based on overall consideration and seeks a balance among the interests of all parties. An incremental reform is one that seeks gradual progress, and it should proceed in a phased manner, starting with the easier issues, and achieve the final objectives of reform through sustained efforts. A result-oriented reform is one that lays emphasis on practical results. All reform measures should contribute to international financial stability and global economic growth as well as the well being of people in all countries."[6] Hu also earnestly proposed four reform measures:

1. Step up international cooperation in financial regulation, improve the international regulatory system, establish codes of conduct for rating agencies, enhance monitoring of global capital flows and regulation of financial institutions and intermediaries of various types, and improve the transparency of financial markets and products.

2. Advance reform of international financial institutions (IFIs). Efforts should be made to reform the mechanisms for formation of their decision-making bodies; increase the representation and voices of developing countries; establish without delay an early-warning system that covers the entire world, especially major international financial centers; improve the internal governance structures of IFIs; put in place a mechanism for swift and efficient crisis response and relief; and enhance the ability of IFIs to fulfill their responsibilities.

3. Encourage regional financial cooperation, enhance the capacity of mutual support in liquidity, develop regional financial infra-structures, and bring into full play the role of regional liquidity assistance mechanisms.

4. Improve the international currency system by steadily promoting its diversification and making joint efforts to support its stability. These are the comprehensive and systematic views from China on the objectives, principles, and measures of international financial system reform.

As a responsible member of the international community, China has always taken an active part in international cooperation to address this crisis and had positive influences on international financial stability and world economic development. In early April 2009, President Hu made the speech entitled "Let Us Join Hands and Tide Over Difficulties Together," and he proposed advancing reform of the international financial system further. He mentioned in particular that international financial institutions should give more assistance to developing countries, that the new funds should be used, first and foremost, to meet the needs of less-developed countries, and that the IMF should strengthen and improve its oversight of the macroeconomic policies of various economies—major reserve-currency-issuing economies in particular, with a special focus on their currency-issuing policies.

Those proposals not only reflect the crucial part of international financial system reform but also present specific ways of operation, which further clears the path to reform the international financial system. To implement and promote the road map of international financial reform, the BRICs—Brazil, Russia, India, and China—took their common stand in the meeting of the G-20 finance ministers and central bank governors in September 2009. They pointed out that governance problems such as unfair distribution of quotas, shares, and voting rights have seriously impacted the legitimacy of the IMF and the World Bank. They stated that the focus of reform should be on a substantial shift of quotas and shares to emerging economies and developing countries. After negotiations and bargains, the countries attending that third G-20 Summit, held in September 2009, agreed to reduce the quotas of European countries in the IMF and the World Bank and to increase the quotas of emerging economies and developing countries by at least 5 percent and the voting rights by at least 3 percent.

Despite that voting reform, developed countries are still in control, with 52 percent and 53 percent of quotas in the IMF and the World Bank, respectively. And as for the United States, its position has never been fundamentally shaken, with its almost 17 percent of the voting rights in the IMF and 16.36 percent in the World Bank. According to the regulations of the IMF and the World Bank, other than exceptions, resolutions cannot be passed without at least half of the voting rights, and significant ones without at least 85 percent. Therefore, the United States still has the virtual veto on significant resolutions.

The reform of the international financial system, which has only just begun, is a long, complex, and gradually advancing process. Though some progress has been achieved in the representation adjustment of international financial institutions, only consensuses have been reached in many other fields, and the G-20 countries still need to work together to promote implementation of the reform objectives and road map. China has always maintained a positive stand, and it will, in a responsible manner, pursue a fair, just, inclusive, and well-managed international economic and financial order through objective and rational consultations and dialogues, with a view to maintain sustainable development of the global economy and establish a harmonious world.

Accelerate Market Opening and Exchange Rate Reform

China's historic changes over the past 30 years are closely related to the Chinese government's persistent adoption of a win-win strategy of opening up and reform. China has actively integrated into the current international system as a participator, adapted to a series of rules formulated by the Western countries, sped up market opening, and successfully achieved sustained and rapid economic development. During the opening up, Chinese government promotes the reasonable and steady reform of the RMB exchange rate while maintaining its stability in accordance with the changing economic situation at home and abroad.

History tells us that no country or economy can avoid currency appreciation pressure while its economy is taking off. And the appropriate solution of the currency issue directly concerns the operation and development of national economy. In the mid-1980s, the United States mobilized the Western European countries to convince Japan, which had a huge trade surplus over the United States, to sign the Plaza Accord. The yen then experienced rapid and sharp appreciation, and the Japanese economy broke down, becoming trapped in a long-term depression. Nowadays, China's situation is just like that of Japan in the 1980s, with a continuing trade surplus and a huge foreign exchange reserve, and RMB appreciation pressure from the United States and other developed countries. Currently, the internal and external problems China faces are more complicated and serious than the ones Japan had at the time.

Manufacturing-based real economy is the foundation of the development of a 1.3-billion population society. Rapid and drastic appreciation of the RMB would not help reduce the trade deficit of the Western countries but on the contrary, would seriously distort the normal track of China's economic development, directly impact export-related industries and business sectors, and therefore lead to rising unemployment and harm the healthy operation of the economy and social harmony and stability. Since 2003, Western countries represented by the United States have kept calling for RMB appreciation. After the outbreak of the international financial crisis in 2008, however, countries throughout the world joined together to fight against its impact, and the issue of RMB appreciation died down.

But in the postcrisis period, Western countries raised the issue of the RMB exchange rate again. In March 2010, both the U.S. Senate and the House of Representatives pressed the Obama administration to list China as a currency manipulator, indicating a mentality of "exchange rate hegemony" held by the United States. This issue is directly related to the misconceptions of Americans who believe that undervaluation of the RMB exchange rate is the main reason for the huge U.S. trade deficit to China. This group believes China takes away job opportunities in the United States and gains unfair competitive advantages with other countries. However, China-U.S. economic and trade exchanges are the results of an international division of labor in economic globalization and have already created a mutually complementary and beneficial situation.

While the U.S. industrial structure is being transformed into a modern service industry, China and other developing countries carry on the traditional labor-intensive industries. The basic reason for China's trade surplus to the United States lies in the low labor and environmental costs in China's market. China's exports to the United States have also actually created huge economic benefits for U.S. consumers. The problem of trade imbalance between China and the United States is due to U.S. export control of high technologies to China, and therefore the trade gap between China and the United States is unable to reflect the real competency gap. In fact, there is no necessary relation between China's sustained trade surplus and the RMB exchange rate.[7] If the RMB appreciates sharply, Western countries will spend more money to import necessary goods made in China, consumers' burden will increase, the trade deficit will probably continue to expand, and enterprises in the Western countries that treat China as a major market will suffer losses. So keeping the RMB exchange rate basically stable at an appropriate and balanced level will benefit the two countries' economic cooperation, bilateral trade, and stable development of the world economy.

According to the semiannual report on international economic and exchange rate policies by the U.S. Treasury Department on July 8, 2010, world total demand decreased by 0.6 percent and China's domestic demand increased by 13 percent, which makes contribution to global economic growth by 1.6 percentage points; China's economic stimulus program promoted U.S. exports to China by 15 percent in the second half of 2009, and U.S. exports to the rest of the world decreased by 13 percent at the same time.

China's attitude toward the RMB exchange rate is rooted in the country's economic and social reality and its profound understanding of the international economy. As a developing country, China regards exchange rate as an important means to regulate the market and the national economy, and its ultimate goal is the sustainable development of the economy and society. So changes in the RMB exchange rate should take into account the country's international trade and balance of payments as well as domestic economic development and are unlikely to be forced to adjust under external pressure. Due to the weak risk-taking capabilities of the financial system and the weak risk absorption of export-oriented enterprises in China, the RMB can appreciate only gradually instead of once and for all. On July 21, 2005, China started to turn to a managed floating exchange rate system based on market supply and demand with reference to a basket of currencies from a fixed one pegged to the U.S. dollar, appreciating the RMB by 2.1 percent. Since the RMB exchange rate reform, the RMB has maintained a steady appreciation process, and the exchange rate of the RMB against the U.S. dollar has appreciated by 20 percent. After the outbreak of the financial crisis, the RMB was pegged to the U.S. dollar again in July 2008, and the central parity rate of the RMB against U.S. dollar has been kept at the level of 6.83 to 6.85. Actually, the RMB exchange rate formation mechanism is an evolving and improving process, and China keeps perfecting the mechanism and keeps the RMB exchange rate basically stable at an appropriate and balanced level in the process, which itself is a contribution to the international community.

The Chinese Government Work Report of 2010 mentioned that "[it will] continue to improve the mechanism for setting the RMB exchange rate and keep it basically stable at an appropriate and balanced level." On April 12, 2010, during the Nuclear Safety Summit in Washington, D.C., Chinese President Hu stressed in his meeting with U.S. president Barack Obama that China would firmly promote the RMB exchange rate formation mechanism, that it was based on China's need for economic and social development, and that the specific measures had to take into consideration world economic development and changes and China's economic operation, which would not be forced to advance under the external pressure. On June 19, 2010, a spokesman for the People's Bank of China said People's Bank of China had decided to further promote reform of the RMB exchange rate formation mechanism and increase the flexibility of the RMB exchange rate according to the domestic and international economic and financial situation and China's international balance of payments.

From now on, China will continue to improve its managed floating exchange rate system based on market supply and demand with reference to a basket of currencies on the principle of an initiative, controllable, and progressive manner in accordance with economic development level, economic situation, and international balance of payments, so as to enable the market to fully play its fundamental role in the formation of the RMB exchange rate and to maintain the RMB exchange rate basically stable—at an appropriate and balanced level.

China and G-20

Global economic issues were once handled by the G-8,[8] a "rich man's club" on behalf of the interests of a very limited group that excluded developing countries. In recent years, the G-8 couldn't solve increasingly prominent global issues and began to invite China, India, and other emerging-market countries to form the mechanism of "G8+5." Although the developing countries get access to the important multilateral platform for dialogues with developed countries on global economic issues, they still don't have the full rights of voice and decision making and are therefore in an unfair position in global economic governance. Since the beginning of the twenty-first century, emerging-market countries have accelerated their rise, with enlarged fields, and have improved the level of their participation in world economic cooperation. Significant changes are taking place in the structure of global governance.

The financial crisis starting in 2007 impacted the international financial order critically and damaged global economic growth. The helplessness of G-8, the IMF, and other international economic organizations and coordination mechanisms controlled by the Western developed countries exposed the severe flaws of the current international economic institutions. The situation brought to light the difficulties the few developed countries faced in dealing with complicated global problems alone. The new international economic realities require emerging-market countries, including China, to play more active roles and to take on appropriate and effective responsibilities in the global governance structure.

The G-20 Summit[9]—an international economic coordination mechanism composed of developed countries, emerging-market countries, and developing countries with relatively high levels of industrialization—was therefore initiated and organized by the United States and other Western powers. From the perspective of participants, G-20 has a decisive influence on the global economy, covering the main economies, two-thirds of the population, 85 percent of GDP, and 80 percent of trade volume in the world. From the perspective of its context, G-20 is the result of the transformation of the international institution caused by the changes in international economic structure in the twenty-first century. Many experts who have researched internal relations between the formation of G-20 and the profound changes in the current international order realize that the improving comprehensive strength of emerging-market countries enables them to be involved in the leadership of global economic governance and transfers a portion of world power from the Atlantic to the Pacific.

There is no doubt that the formation and development of the G-20 mechanism reflect the latest development in the present world economic pattern. These changes contribute to the promotion of the decision-making mechanism for global affairs to a more diversified, balanced, and effective direction and are conducive to developing countries' pursuit of a new international economic order that would be fair and reasonable. Since its first summit in Washington in November 2008, G-20 has held four important summits and reached extensive consensus on promoting world economic recovery and international financial system reform, enhancing financial supervision, and rebalancing the global economy, which is efficient and fruitful. Especially in the third summit in Pittsburgh, the participating countries issued the Leader's Declaration, stating that the G-20 was institutionalized with a summit once a year from 2011 and became the major platform of international economic cooperation and coordination instead of G-8.

China regards opening up and taking part in international cooperation, in an all-directional manner, as an important part of its foreign strategy. Active participation in the G-20 mechanism is in conformity with China's strategy of peaceful development. Early in the "G8+5" mechanism, China had gradually participated in the process of global policy coordination. Relatively limited as its influence was, it had achieved positive progress to consult with developed countries as a developing country and to express China's policy positions and attitudes on major international affairs. G-20 is not a replacement of G-8 but a type of natural succession and expansion. Its establishment and development provide a broad platform for China to take part in international cooperation at a higher level and to participate in international dialogues and cooperation more equally, which helps improve China's voice and influence in international economic affairs.

China advocates dialogues and cooperation instead of conflicts and confrontations to solve international problems. International cooperation calls for participants to perform their responsibilities and obligations proactively and to maintain the overall situation. In the framework of G-20, to deal with the financial crisis, China has voluntarily fulfilled its obligations, persisted in advancing reform of the international financial system, and put forth a series of constructive proposals to promote the world economy for strong, sustainable, and balanced growth.

The G-20 should stand firm in its commitment to stimulating economic growth. The Chinese government pays lots of attention to the G-20 mechanism and advocates making full use of the platform to step up macroeconomic policy coordination while maintaining the overall consistency and the timely and forward-looking nature of policies. In order to ensure economic growth in the financial crisis, the Chinese government has maintained the strength of economic stimulus packages effectively and made greater efforts to boost consumption and expand domestic demand, which has contributed to world economic recovery as it achieved the intended growth goal.

The G-20 should also stand firm in its commitment to advancing the reform of the international financial system. The Chinese government believes that the political consensus on reforming the international financial system—which the G-20 leaders reached—is a solemn promise to the entire world. They should not shatter their determination or lower their sights because of the improved international economic situation but instead ought to work on it continuously.

The G-20 should stand firm in its commitment to promoting balanced growth of the global economy. The current global economic imbalance is manifested mainly in imbalances between savings and consumption and between imports and exports in some countries, as well as imbalances in global wealth distribution, resource availability, consumption, and the international monetary system. The Chinese government stands for the perfection of international mechanisms that promote balanced development, support of the United Nations in better guidance and coordination of development efforts, and encouragement of the World Bank to increase development resources and enhance its role in poverty reduction and economic development. China also supports exerting pressure on the IMF to set up a financial rescue mechanism that would provide prompt and effective assistance and give financing support to the least-developed countries on a priority basis.[10] Since the financial crisis, China has delivered assistance to developing countries in various ways and channels, including:

- Replenishing US$50 billion to the IMF and clearly requiring the IMF to allocate more resources to the least-developed countries
- Signing bilateral currency swap agreements of 650 billion RMB with other countries and regions
- Providing credit supports of US$10 billion for other members of the Shanghai Cooperation Organization
- Providing preferential loans of US$10 billion for African countries
- Canceling the debts owed by the heavily indebted poor countries and the least-developed countries in Africa
- Gradually exempting tariffs for 95 percent of the products of the least-developed countries in Africa that have diplomatic relations with China

China believes that the G-20 should be transformed from an effective mechanism for countering the international financial crisis to a major platform for advancing international economic cooperation. The Chinese government holds that G-20 should play a guiding role in promoting international economic cooperation and global economic governance. It believes that the focus of the G-20 should be shifted from coordinating stimulus measures to coordinating growth, from addressing short-term contingencies to promoting long-term governance, and from passive response to proactive planning. Countries should uphold together the credibility and effectiveness of the G-20, advance the institutional buildup of G-20 under the principle of seeking gradual progress and win-win outcomes, and properly handle various problems and differences in order to ensure sound development of the G-20 summit mechanism.[11]

Currently, the international community has a high expectation of G-20 in addressing the financial crisis and promoting global economic recovery. G-20 should embody more predictability instead of defensiveness and conservatism, but its development prospect is still uncertain. China and other developing countries try to promote G-20 to be an important platform for the international economic system reform, but they are only participants, and the United States and other Western countries are the real dominators who have key influence on the operation and development of the G-20 mechanism. With the shrinking gap of strength between the Western countries and the emerging-market countries, it is imperative for the future of G-20 that the world's economic decision-making rights be smoothly transferred from a Western-led pattern to a relatively balanced and multilateral one.

China and the Doha Round

The *Doha Round* refers to the new round of global multilateral trade negotiations launched in the Fourth World Trade Organization (WTO) Ministerial Conference in Doha, Qatar, in November 2001, covering issues involving agriculture, nonagricultural market access, service trade, rules negotiations, trade and development, dispute settlement, intellectual property rights, and trade and environment, among which agriculture issues are at the core. Doha Round negotiations aim at reducing trade barriers, improving global trade rule, and promoting balanced development in the world, especially in developing countries. The Doha Round is the first round of multilateral trade negotiations after the establishment of the WTO in 1995 and also the round with the most participators and subjects on the agenda since the establishment of the multilateral trade system. It is of great significance to the promotion of free trade and global economic growth. According to the assessment report of the World Bank, the successful completion of the Doha Round will make a contribution of US$150 billion to global economic growth every year. However, relevant members of the WTO cannot reach agreement on the distribution of core interests, and thus the negotiations—which should have been finished in January 1, 2005—broke down several times, and no concrete results have ensued. Members' disagreements focus on the three core issues of agricultural subsidies and tariff reductions for agricultural and nonagricultural products.

The current global trade system was founded and is led by developed countries; developing countries are always in a passive and vulnerable position, which directly causes unfair consequences in international trade. The Doha Round is a complicated bargaining process for interests' adjustment. In recent years, the strength balance among the participants has changed with the continuously improving strength of emerging-market countries and developing countries and their increasing rights of speech on the formulation and adjustment of multilateral trade rules, which leads to the weakened ability of Western powers to control the negotiations alone. In this situation, the competition around vital interests between developed countries and developing ones will become more complex and intense. Developing countries hope that developed ones reduce tariffs on agricultural products and the trade-distorting agricultural subsidies, eliminate unfair and unreasonable trade rules, and at the same time care more for less-advanced countries' abilities to perform responsibilities in multilateral negotiations. Developing countries also hope for greater autonomy to protect their domestic industries.

But developed countries still ignore the "special and different treatment" and "special safeguards" raised by developing countries; keep keen on market access, trade, and environment and labor standards; and require that developing countries open their nonagricultural markets further. The nine-year experience of the Doha Round indicates that the structural contradictions between developed and developing countries are the primary causes of its delays, and it shows the difference and diversity of development of WTO members and their profound differences in the international trade operation and rules. After the outbreak of the international financial crisis of 2008, the international community's expectation for the Doha Round of negotiations has increased as the agreements will act as strong stimulants to the gloomy world economy. With the rise of international trade protectionism, however, as well as the "consensus" principle and the "package" negotiation approach of the WTO and related complicated political, economic, and technical problems, the prospects for global multilateral trade negotiations are still not optimistic.

China's rapid development benefits from the increasing scale and level of foreign trade. Since it acceded to WTO in 2001, China has proactively learned and adapted to the global multilateral trade rules, taken chances to participate in and make use of the multilateral trade institutions and to fulfill its commitments and obligations, and supported global free trade. As reported in July 2010, "By 2010, China has fully fulfilled its promises made when joining WTO and established the economic and trade system meeting the regulatory requirements, becoming one of the most open markets in the world."[12] Taking part in globalization actively, China is not only a participant in the world economic rules but also a promoter and builder of the new rules and order. China recognizes that concrete results of the Doha Round are helpful to form institutional constraints for trade protectionism and to establish a just and reasonable international trade system. China is firmly supportive of the advancement of the negotiation process and holds a view that the target of negotiations should contribute to (1) the establishment of a new international economic order that is fair, just, and reasonable; (2) the sustainable economic development and facilitation of trade and investment in the world; and (3) balanced economic development in the world.

Since China joined WTO negotiations and consultations at the ministerial and senior official levels, it has taken part in negotiations on the core issues of agriculture as well as negotiations in other fields such as nonagriculture, service, and rules, submitting over 100 proposals. It is important to note that as a new member that has committed and fulfilled higher-level obligations, China has still expressed its attitude of refusing the "free lunch," making new commitments of free trade, and opening the domestic goods and services market, and that it bears in mind overall interests as a proactive and responsible participator in global trade.[13] From 1992 to 2007, China's nonagricultural tariffs decreased from 42 percent to 8.9 percent, by a rate of 80 percent. Agricultural tariffs fell from 54 percent before joining the WTO to 15.3 percent in 2007; the world average rate of tariffs on agricultural products was 62 percent at the same time.

With the outbreak of the financial crisis of 2008, China made unremitting efforts on the restoration and promotion of the Doha Round to conclude the negotiations early and to reduce the discriminatory rules of the global multilateral trade system for developing countries. In the UN conference on responses to the financial crisis in December 2008, China illuminated its proposal of restraining trade protectionism and promoting positive progress in the Doha Round. In 2009, in order to break the deadlock, the Chinese government raised the principles of "consistent with its mandate, locking in the progress already made and basing the negotiations on the existing texts," which were acknowledged and supported by most of the members and reflected in the two declarations of the G-20 Summit. On September 3, 2009, Chinese minister of commerce Chen Deming proposed five suggestions on promoting the Doha Round at the WTO Mini-ministerial Conference in New Delhi, India:

1. The world should protect outcomes of the negotiations and the flexibility acquired by developing countries, especially the principles of the autonomy of developing members to designate special agricultural products and of the voluntary participation in nonagricultural "sector concessions," which was the consensus reached by all parties and should be respected.
2. Though the international community is not against improving understandings about each other by bilateral consultations, the core channel of promoting negotiations should consist of multilateral approaches.
3. The G-20 should follow the order of finishing agricultural and nonagricultural sectors first.
4. The G-20 should adhere to the combination of negotiation process and quality and pursue a balanced and reasonable result.
5. The G-20 should adhere to the purpose of the Doha Round, which is to resolve specific concerns of developing countries, especially the least-developed ones.

At present and in the coming period, as a new member of the WTO, China still has to improve its understanding and application of multilateral trade rules and its experience in multilateral trade negotiations. These all will be achieved in China's deeper and wider participation in multilateral trade. There is no doubt that China always holds the basic principle of "mutual benefit" and is a strong supporter of the multilateral trade system, an important upholder of free-trade principles, and an active promoter of the Doha Round so as to advance globalization in the direction of balance, mutual benefit, and win-win.

Global Economic Imbalance and China's Endogenous Capacity Building

The worsening global economic imbalance since the advent of the twenty-first century is the root cause of the financial crisis. One important manifestation of the imbalance is the U.S. dollar's hegemony and the worsening current account and expanding external debts caused by domestic overconsumption. Meanwhile, emerging-market countries and petroleum-exporting countries have depended on export for a long time to develop the economy and have accumulated a huge number of trade surpluses and dollar reserves. The imbalance of the global economy reflects the irrationality of the current international economic order and monetary system. Developing countries are in a passive and dependent status. After the breakout of the global financial crisis, a sharp drop in imports by the European and American countries and the rise of trade protectionism led to China's worsening foreign trade environment. According to the statistics of China's Ministry of Commerce, China's products were involved in 101 trade remedy investigations by 19 countries and regions from January to November 2009, and US$11.68 billion was involved, an increase of 639 percent year on year. China became a WTO member with the most antisubsidy investigations in the world as well.

With the development of emerging-market countries, China will meet more-powerful challenges in manufacturing and export. The financial crisis, on one hand, highlights the problem with China's economic structure and on the other hand provides opportunities to accelerate its adjustment. In the new situation, China's government should actively face challenges and adjust its general thoughts. It should aim at enhancing endogenous capacity building and speeding up the development strategy transformation, so as to switch the economic development strategy from export-oriented to domestic-demand growth.

Since 2008, the Chinese government has taken measures on infrastructure construction, people's livelihood protection, domestic-demand expansion, and employment promotion, which "reflects the thoughts from 'dealing with emergency' to 'long-term considerations' and then back to the 'essence of growth' and scientific development.'"[14] At the end of 2008, the Chinese government launched a 4-trillion-RMB investment program on infrastructure and livelihood projects (Table 5.1), together with a proactive fiscal policy and a moderately easy monetary policy. It emphasized fast and forceful acts and accurate and

Table 5.1 The 4-Trillion-RMB Investment Program Involving Infrastructure and Livelihood Projects (Unit: Billion)

	Original Plan	After Adjustment	Proportion
Railway, Road, Airport, and Electrical Network	1,800	1,500	37.5%
Affordable Housing	280	400	10%
Technological Transformation and Structural Adjustment	160	370	9.25%
Rural Livelihood and Infrastructure	370	370	9.25%
Medical Health Service, Culture and Education and Society	40	150	3.75%
Energy Saving and Environment	350	210	5.25%
Reconstruction of Stricken Areas	1,000	1,000	25%

Source: National Development and Reform Commission of the People's Republic of China.

practical measures and promoted economic growth through expansion of government investment in public construction. The growth rate of GDP in 2008 was 9 percent.

After realizing the goal of ensuring growth, China's government has gradually shifted its focus to "adjusting the structure, expanding domestic demand, and benefiting livelihood." Compared with investment and export, consumption is always the "shot slab" among the troika for China's economic growth. Impacted by the financial crisis, the global supply and demand structure and trade pattern are changing profoundly, and China's mode of economic development, which is highly dependent on external demand, faces increasing adjustment pressure.

Since 2009, in order to make up for inadequate endogenous growth power, China's government has taken a series of measures to expand domestic demand, especially consumer demand, including implementing subsidies on household electrical appliances and cars to the countryside and old to new, accelerating the income distribution reform, and improving the income of low-income groups. In November 2009, the State Council issued 10 policies to expand domestic demand and promote balanced and rapid economic growth—namely, the "economic stimulus package." It mainly consists of speeding up construction of affordable housing projects, rural infrastructure and railways, roads, airports, and other major infrastructure; speeding up medical, health, cultural, and educational development; strengthening ecological environment construction; speeding up innovation and structural adjustment; accelerating the reconstruction of quake-hit areas; increasing the incomes of urban and rural residents; starting the value-added-tax reform in all regions and industries all over the country; encouraging technological upgrading of enterprises; and increasing financial support for economic growth.

Seen from the program content point of view, China's coping with the financial crisis is not simply emergency processing but is also aimed at promoting innovation and social welfare, solving structural problems obstructing China's economic development for the long term, and improving the comprehensive competitiveness and quality of the national economy by implementation of adjustment projects for industries and economic structure.[15] "The package is a complete and integrated program, that is, a program to take into account the immediate and future situations and to mobilize both the central and local enthusiasm by the two hands of market and macro-control."[16]

China has also made primary achievements on enhancing endogenous capacity in the situation of global economic imbalance and is the first to achieve the goal of stable economic recovery among the biggest economies of the world. Its GDP growth rate in 2009 was 8.7 percent, ranking first in the world. In 2010, GDP reached 10.3 percent, followed by 9.3 percent in 2011 and 7.8 percent in 2012. However, it is undeniable that it is extremely difficult for China to transform its economic development mode from investment oriented to consumption oriented fundamentally in a short time, as its economic development faces very complicated contradictions that have existed for a long time. The Chinese government has formed a series of policy ideas on adjusting economic structure and improving economic growth quality and efficiency and will implement them soon. The ideas mainly include tasks in the following key aspects:

- **Adjustment of demand structure.** The government will enhance the economic-stimulus effect of consumption while maintaining moderate growth in investment and stabilizing external demand.
- **Adjustment of income distribution structure.** The government will improve the proportion of labor remuneration in the primary distribution of income and narrow the income gap.
- **Adjustment of industrial structure.** The government should focus on improving the proportion of service industry at the same time as it strengthens agriculture's fundamental role and encourages industries to grow stronger.
- **Adjustment of the structure within industries.** On one hand, the government will eliminate backward industrial production capacity; on the other hand, it will make efforts to cultivate new industries.

- **Adjustment of the urban-rural structure.** The government will take pains over the urbanization and integration of urban and rural development as well as continue to strengthen rural development.
- **Adjustment of the regional economic structure.** The government will keep on following the overall regional development strategy for a new pattern of complementary advantages, positive interaction, and coordinated development.
- **Adjustment of the spatial structure of land development.** The government will promote the construction of primary functional areas.
- **Adjustment of the foreign trade structure.** The government will raise the export proportion of products of general trade and own brand.[17]

Although the global economy continues to recover slowly, problems in the international financial system have yet to be solved and there are still uncertain and unstable factors at play. China will rely on its own strength and development experience by focusing its policies on the overall expansion of domestic demand, so as to soon form a pattern of economic growth driven mainly by domestic demand and active use of external demand; thus the economy will become more balanced and rational. In the next period, China will deepen reform content constantly through innovation of ideas, institutions, and policies, and it will promote adjustment of the economic structure and improve the quality of economic development further through the enhancement of endogenous capacity building. Therefore, it will provide more-powerful support for global economic recovery and development.

Expansion of New Energy Path

In September 2009, at the UN Climate Change Summit, President Hu earnestly claimed that China's consumption of nonfossil energy would account for 15 percent of the country's total energy consumption by 2020. In December 2009, at the Copenhagen Climate Change Conference, Premier Wen Jiabao made a commitment to the world that the carbon dioxide emission of one unit of GDP in 2020 would be decreased by 40 to 45 percent compared with that in 2005 and that the emission reduction targets would be included in the plan for national economic and social development as mandatory targets. And he promised that the implementation would be supervised by law and the public. That commitment reflects that China is actively taking international responsibility for global governance, and it indicates that new changes will take place in China's energy consumption structure. China will continue to expand the new energy path firmly in the stage of rapid industrialization.

Energy forms the material basis of survival and development for a modern country. With the rapid and sustaining development of its economy and its society, China is dramatically in want of energy. However, China faces a worsening energy shortage due to the limited total amount, the low amount per capita, the irrational energy structure of "being rich in coal, poor in oil, and lacking in gas," and high rates of foreign dependency. For example, in 2009, China produced 189 million tons of crude oil whereas net import of crude oil was as high as 199 million tons. The crude oil import dependency is 51.29 percent, which was over the warning line of 50 percent for the first time. China has low energy efficiency and excessive pollutant emission. At present, coal still dominates China's energy consumption. In the long term, China cannot improve its energy structure without rapid development of renewable energy and new energy. With adjustment of the industrial structure, the popularization of new techniques, and the implementation of policies for new energy, the proportion of new energy in China's overall energy consumption has been gradually increasing.

In the utilization of solar energy, solar water heaters represent the earliest and one of the largest renewable energy industries in China. Now ownership of solar water heaters has become 125 million square meters, accounting for 70 percent of the world. And China has achieved rapid development in solar photovoltaic as a photoelectric conversion device. The production of photovoltaic products amounted to 2.5 million kilowatts in 2008, or 35 percent of the world.

In the utilization of wind energy, China has nearly 1 billion kilowatts of wind energy, according to statistics, and a promising future of development and utilization. Its wind energy development is approaching industrialization, with 12 million kilowatts of total installed capacity in 2008. China became one of the countries with wind power installed capacity of over 10 million kilowatts, ranking first in Asia and fourth in the world.

In nuclear power, according to the China Electricity Council, China's total installed capacity of nuclear power was 9.08 million kilowatts, and generated nuclear power, 70 billion kilowatts by the end of 2009. Bloomberg New Energy Finance said that China's new financial investment in wind power totaled US$21.8 billion in 2009, a rise of 27 percent over the previous year and in that investment solar energy was US$1.9 billion, a rise of 97 percent. China has become the second-biggest country in the world in investment in renewable energy, after the United States, followed by Germany. The rapid development of new energy promotes the gradual optimization of energy structure in China. In the domestic primary energy consumption structure of 2009, coal accounted for 68.7 percent, oil for 18 percent, and natural gas for 3.4 percent, and renewable energy rose to 9.9 percent.

The Chinese Government Work Report of 2010 stated clearly it would "make efforts on low carbon technology, popularization of the efficient and energy-saving technology, development of new energy and renewable energy and the construction of smart grid." To promote the new energy industry, the government continues to improve relevant laws and institutions. In January 2010, the State Council formed the National Energy Commission (NEC), which works out the national energy development strategy, reviews major issues in energy security and development, and coordinates significant affairs in domestic energy development and international energy cooperation. Premier Wen serves as director of the NEC. The establishment of the NEC will help cross-sectional and cross-industrial cooperation at a higher level and jointly solve problems in energy development, so as to speed up the low-carbon economy. On April 1, 2010, the Amendment to the Renewable Energy Law came into effect, aiming to advance the development and utilization of renewable energy, increase energy supply, improve energy structure, protect the environment, and realize sustainable development of the economy and society. "The amendment will benefit the elimination of low-quality production as well as lay the legal foundation for the goal of energy saving and emission reduction."[18]

China has set its long- and medium-term programs of promoting new energy development now, and it will soon issue an "emerging energy industry development plan" from 2011 to 2020. On July 20, 2010, Jiang Bing, director of the Planning and Development Division of the National Energy Board, said that the basic assumption of energy development is to take effective measures to save energy and improve the clean utilization of traditional energy and at the same time to develop alternative industries and increase the scale of natural gas and other clean energies. And the government will optimize energy structure through the construction of hydropower, nuclear power projects, and the utilization of renewable energy, including wind, solar, and biomass energy.

According to the energy plan in the 12th Five-Year Plan, by 2015 the utilization scale of natural gas will be 260 billion cubic meters, and its proportion in the energy consumption structure will be increased to around 8.3 percent; the scale of hydropower and nuclear power will be 250 million kilowatts and 39 million kilowatts, respectively, accounting for 9 percent of primary energy consumption; the scale of other, nonhydro renewable energy will be 110 million tons of standard coal, and the proportion will be about 2.6 percent. At that time, the proportion of nonfossil energy in primary energy consumption is expected to be 11 percent, and by 2020, 15 percent. It is estimated that after implementation of the emerging energy industry plan, China will experience a significant reduction in its overreliance on coal demand by 2020 and that emissions of sulfur dioxide and carbon dioxide will reduce by about 7.8 million tons and 1.2 billion tons, respectively, in that year. According to the strategic road map of China's energy technology development by the Chinese Academy of Sciences, recent focus (from the present to 2020) is on the technology of energy saving and clean energy and on the improvement of energy efficiency; the medium-term focus (around 2030) will be on the development of nuclear energy and renewable energy to the major energy; the long-term focus (around 2050) will be on the establishment of China's sustainable energy system, which will basically meet the energy demand of China's economic and social development, of which dependence on fossil energy will fall below 60 percent and in which renewable energy will be one of the major energies.

In the global emission reduction of greenhouse gases, the international community ought to take responsibility together. The Western developed countries have the obligation to help developing countries in capital and technology. But the developed countries get used to restraining the export of advanced technology and management experience to developing countries. Therefore, China has to develop new energy by enhancing international cooperation based on self-reliance. As much effort as China has made on new energy development, its investment in basic research and development is obviously insufficient; no great breakthrough has ever been made in key technologies; and the application and management of new energy technologies are still backward compared with international advanced levels. China will make great efforts to improve the innovation ability of energy technology and enhance the construction of modern energy systems. China will also continue the strategy of going global, deepen its international energy cooperation, and expand the space of external energy cooperation.

Case Study—Regional Integration in East Asia

Active participation in regional integration in East Asia is one of the important manifestations of China's active integration into the international system. After the outbreak of a financial crisis in Southeast Asia, East Asia sped up regional cooperation in the spirit of regionalism. China also joined in the East Asia integration based on its own situation of rapid economic development and increasingly closer relations between East Asian countries. Then the Troika mechanism was formed, consisting of the Association of Southeast Asian Nations (ASEAN) and China (10+3), ASEAN and China, Japan and the Republic of Korea and the East Asia Summit. And a series of operating mechanisms including leaders' summits, ministers' councils, and senior officials meetings has been established.

China adheres to policies of friendship and partnership with neighboring countries and harmony, security, and prosperity for neighbors in its participation in East Asian integration. It accepts the concept of "open regionalism" and refuses closed groups. It maintains and develops cooperation with countries and regions outside East Asia with an inclusive attitude. After its participation in the regional integration, dialogues and coordination between East Asian countries and regions have been extraordinarily developed with continuous enhancement and great improvement. A new situation of interdependence and cooperation between the economies has formed, and the status of East Asia has kept on rising in the world.

China respects ASEAN's leading role in East Asian integration and takes active part in cooperation at all levels and in all fields. ASEAN is the forerunner and inner driving force of East Asian cooperation. Since its establishment in 1967, it has made efforts for regional economic exchange and trade investment and the construction of internal institutions and has achieved much significant progress. It also launched the East Asian Cooperation Framework after the financial crisis in Southeast Asia in 1997. As Zheng Xianwu reported in 2009, "As there is still no unified organizational structure of East Asian regionalism, it just relies on the existing ASEAN and thus the acknowledged East Asian regionalism becomes the mechanism for ASEAN-centered subregional and interregional collective dialogue and cooperation."[19]

In official documents, ASEAN countries also stress the core position of ASEAN in the Troika mechanism. Since the acceleration of economic cooperation with Southeast Asian countries in the 1990s, China has always acted as a participant and collaborator in East Asian integration, supporting ASEAN's leading role in the integration and the "ASEAN Way" and "ASEAN Norms" as expressed in the East Asia cooperation mechanism. After China became a full dialogue partner of ASEAN in 1996, it started communication and cooperation on international, regional, political, economic, and security problems with ASEAN countries and other dialogue partners. In the financial crisis of Southeast Asia in 1997, China actively performed the responsibilities of a great power and decided not to depreciate the RMB, playing a vital role in maintaining the stability of East Asia and promoting economic recovery. The ASEAN Regional Forum is the most important ASEAN-led multilateral security dialogue mechanism in the Asian and Pacific regions. And China always takes an active part in its activities and holds dialogues with related countries on regional security situations and nontraditional security issues.

In October 2003, China took the lead in participating in the Treaty of Amity and Cooperation in Southeast Asia as a power outside ASEAN, and politically mutual trust between China and ASEAN countries deepened.

China also supports trade liberalization in East Asia and promotes innovation of new institutions and the development of existing ones. Since the 1980s, with the deepening interdependence between countries and regions, institutionalism has had a substantial influence on the international community, and the institution and mechanisms have been important forms and security of cooperation among countries and regions. At present, global multilateral trade talks have been slow, but close regional economic links have been formed in East Asia, with increasing cooperation mechanisms and rapid development of free-trade-area networks. In 2000, China proposed a China-ASEAN Free Trade Area formally. In November 2002, China officially signed the Framework Agreement on China-ASEAN Comprehensive Economic Co-operation with ASEAN and decided to complete the establishment of a free-trade zone before 2010. (The deadline for new members of ASEAN is in 2015.) Under China's promotion, the two parties continued signing a Trade in Goods Agreement in November 2004, a General Agreement on Trade in Services in January 2007, and an Investment Agreement in August 2009.

On January 1, 2010, a huge free-trade area was formally launched with nearly US$6 trillion of GDP and US$4.5 trillion of trade volume.

In this zone, over 7,000 kinds of goods are at zero tariff; China's average tariff on ASEAN members dropped from 9.8 percent to 0.1 percent; and the average tariff of the six old members of ASEAN—Indonesia, Malaysia, Singapore, Thailand, the Philippines, and Brunei—on China also dropped—from 12.8 percent to 0.6 percent. According to those agreements, Myanmar, Cambodia, Laos, and Vietnam—the four new members of ASEAN—will join in this free-trade area in 2015. Since the launch of the free-trade area, the bilateral trade value between China and ASEAN has reached US$136.49 billion, up 54.7 percent. China's exports to ASEAN member amount to US$64.6 billion, up 45.4 percent; its imports are US$71.89 billion, up 64 percent. Now ASEAN has surpassed Japan to become China's third-largest trading partner. It has also become the third-biggest free-trade area in the world, after the European Union and North America.

The Chinese government has a positive attitude toward the construction of a free-trade area of 10+1. It advocates that China and ASEAN carry out the agreements carefully; insist on open-market and -trade and -investment facilitation; enhance their industrial cooperation and scientific and technical innovation; and oppose all kinds of protectionism. Yang Jiechi, China's minister of foreign affairs, expressed that "China will continue to support the building of ASEAN Community through bilateral and multilateral channels" and reaffirmed that "ASEAN should maintain centrality in East Asian cooperation."[20]

China upholds open regionalism other than self-isolation or exclusive groups, and it supports dialogues between countries of 10+3 as well as outside countries and organizations. In October 2003, the Joint Declaration of the Heads of State/Government of the People's Republic of China and the Member States of ASEAN on Strategic Partnership for Peace and Prosperity made it clear that the bilateral partnership is nonalliance, nonmilitary, and nonexclusive; does not direct against any third party; and respects the legitimate interests of the United States and other outside countries in East Asia.

With the rising status of East Asia in the U.S. global strategy, President Obama has adjusted the East Asia policy of the United States.

Since 2009, Obama has stressed that the United States is a pacific country and "taking part in ASEAN" is "one of the most significant parts of the general approach" of the United States. In 2009, besides the Treaty of Amity and Cooperation in Southeast Asia, the United States also established a leaders' summit with ASEAN, a "10+1" between ASEAN and the United States. China's international cooperation view is open and inclusive and therefore not against cooperation between the United States and ASEAN. It welcomes the United States to support regional integration in East Asia and to play a constructive and beneficial role in the peace and development of East Asia.

The establishment of a cooperation mechanism between China and ASEAN has laid a firm foundation for East Asian Community. Chinese vice president Xi Jinping said in a Japan and Republic of Korea joint interview in Beijing in December 2009 that this idea is consistent with the trend of Asian integration and that that is the common goal of the countries in this region, including China and Japan. He said that East Asia Community is a systemic project, so we have to base it on reality and have a long-term perspective, and the most important thing now is to enhance dialogues between countries and forge a consensus.[21] According to this idea, China promoted financial cooperation in East Asia through the multilateralism in the Chiang Mai Initiative and assumed the share of US$38.4 billion in the East Asian foreign exchange reserve, which not only strengthened the ability to withstand financial risks in this region but also made an important contribution to the construction of East Asian Community.

China's participation in the integration of East Asia is not only the definite choice of China—which adheres to a policy of opening up and peaceful development—but also an important manifestation that China is ready to undertake the responsibilities of an Asia-Pacific regional power. China will continue to actively participate in promoting regional integration in East Asia with an open and collaborative attitude, so as to realize common prosperity through cooperation.

CHINA'S RESPONSIBLE AND CONSTRUCTIVE ROLE IN THE INTERNATIONAL COMMUNITY

Since introduction of the reform and opening-up policy, China has gradually formed a new view of the international community; that is, China must actively participate in international economic and technological cooperation and learn from all the outstanding achievements of human civilization in order to achieve the goal of socialist modernization. Under the guidance of this concept, China has made the strategic choice of fully integrating into the international community, which means that on one hand, China will promote domestic development through fully attracting foreign capital and advanced technologies and management skills, and on the other hand, China will step by step get rid of its national identity as an outsider of the international system, become a responsible member of the international community, make contributions to the international community despite its daunting task of domestic development, and seek a harmonious world of permanent peace and common prosperity.

The concept of the free ride exists in any human organization. Simply put, it refers to the action of one member's enjoyment of the benefits provided by an organization but who demonstrates reluctance or unwillingness to pay the shared costs of participation. The pioneer of the theory, American economist Mancur Olson, contended that the root of the free ride is that personal efforts would not have obvious effects on the organization, so regardless of one's contributions to the organization one would still enjoy the benefits brought about by others.[1] Therefore, as a huge country, China is unable and unwilling to have a free ride. This is reflected in the relationship between China and the international economic system.

China's economic achievements have indeed benefited from globalization, but its huge size determines that the realization of its development needs is sure to impose positive effects on the international community. Therefore, it is impossible objectively for China to become a free rider in the international community. By the end of 2008, China's total imports and exports had reached US$1,132.56 billion and US$1,430.69 billion, respectively, surpassing Germany to become the world's largest exporter (Figure 6.1).

Though both of China's import and export volumes decreased, totaling US$1201.66 billion in 2009 because of the financial crisis, China is still the world's largest exporter. In terms of the use of foreign capital, from 1979 to 2006 total actual foreign investments in China amounted to US$876.226 billion (Figure 6.2), and actual total use of foreign direct investments reached US$685.437 billion (Figure 6.3).

On the other hand, rapid growth in China's foreign trade and the foreign investments it has attracted are, in the final analysis, based on the development needs of 1.3 billion people. In other words, China on one hand is bound to enjoy the benefits of globalization for its own development but on the other hand provides a market based on the world's largest population, actively promoting worldwide industrial

Figure 6.1 Growth Trend of China's Value of Foreign Trade (1978–2008)

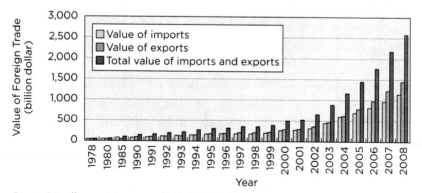

Source: http://www. stats. gov. cn/tjsj/ndsj/2009/indexch. htm.

Figure 6.2 Foreign Investments in China (1979–2006)

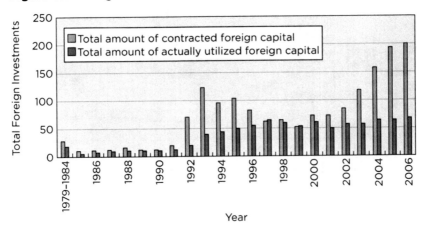

Source: http://www.stats.gov.cn/tjsj/ndsj/2009/indexch.htm.

Figure 6.3 Total Foreign Direct Investments in China (1979–2006)

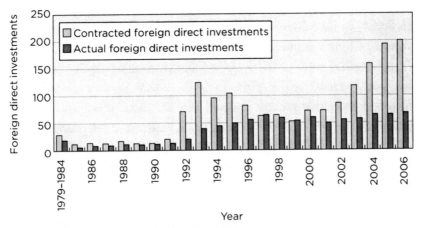

Source: http://www.stats.gov.cn/tjsj/ndsj/2009/indexch.htm.

relocation and restructure and building a solid economic foundation for the international community.

The most typical example is the financial plan of about 4 trillion RMB (about US$586 billion) launched by the Chinese government during the 2008 financial crisis. The plan not only effectively stimulated domestic demand but also made an important contribution to the recovery of the world economy. As Figure 6.4 shows—driven

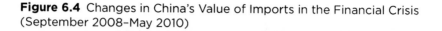

Figure 6.4 Changes in China's Value of Imports in the Financial Crisis (September 2008–May 2010)

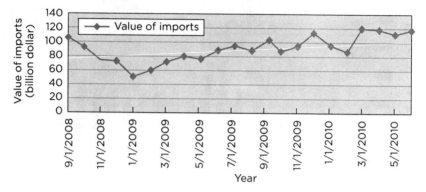

Source: Based on statistics provided by China Customs,http://www.customs.gov.cn/publish/portal0/tab4370/module3760/page3.htm.

by domestic demand, from September 2008, when the financial crisis began, to June 2010—despite the sharp falls and fluctuations in the value of China's imports, the overall trend was upward.

China has undoubtedly played an important role in stabilizing the world market in the crisis. Facts show that China's contribution to world economic growth reached over 20 percent in 2008 and surpassed 50 percent in 2009. On this basis, China is accelerating its step of formulating measures to encourage imports. The first service platform for promoting imports—the Shanghai Imported Commodities Exhibition and Trade Center was officially established in Pudong, Shanghai, and on August 2, 2012, the International Import Commodity Exhibition Trade Center officially settled in Shanghai. This key project is one of many created by cooperation between Shanghai Municipality and the Ministry of Commerce. The project is also an important action toward promoting trade balance, dealing in imported goods, in which Shanghai will work closely with governments of other countries or districts globally.

Enjoying the benefits of globalization and promoting globalization are actually two sides of a coin for China. As China is experiencing an unprecedented large-scale emergence in human history,[2] it must have a strong domestic demand. While in the contemporary world of deepening interdependence that domestic need will necessarily become an important part of the world market, so that China is sure to make contributions to building the international community while enjoying the benefits of globalization.

From the subjective perspective, China itself hopes to make contributions to building the international community. First, China always positions itself as a big power and adheres to the principle of reciprocity of "rights, responsibilities, and interests." Each top leader of the government of the People's Republic of China has publicly stated that "China is a big power and should contribute to the world," indicating that China has never evaded its responsibilities, but the opposite: it is willing to take the initiative to bear responsibility. *Spider-Man* is a world-famous American film in which one classic line is "Great power comes with great responsibility." Since Spider-Man has superpower, he ought to fight against the evil and protect the weak. The success of this film in China undoubtedly indicates that this Western value has also received recognition in Chinese society. One of the reasons is the culture of chivalry in the genes of the Chinese, meaning that those good at martial arts should punish evil and uphold justice. Jin Yong, a famous martial arts novelist in Hong Kong, has created many such righteous heroes in his masterpieces popular in the Chinese world. Therefore, "Great power comes with great responsibility" is a common value connecting Eastern and Western societies.

At the national level, China never evades its responsibilities because of its status of a big power. On the other hand, "Great power comes with great responsibility" also connotes the principle of equivalence between abilities, responsibilities, and rights. In other words, "great power" is the premise of "great responsibility." If one must assume responsibilities beyond one's ability, one could not save others at all but, rather, would have to be saved by others. Such is the case in China. Although its ability has been significantly increased compared with that in the past, and correspondingly it should shoulder—and has shouldered—many international responsibilities, after all, China has not got rid of the basic characteristics of a developing country.

Therefore, most of its GDP of US$5 trillion and foreign exchange reserves of US$2 trillion have to be used to meet the need of domestic development. This determines fundamentally that China's primary responsibility must be the success of internal governance—and then can come limited foreign responsibilities. Simultaneously, China must resolutely defend its legal rights and realize the unity of "rights, responsibilities, and interests."

Second, China is willing to make contributions to stabilizing the international community in order to create a favorable environment for peaceful development. British scholar Hedley Bull was well-known for his studies on the international community in anarchy. In his view, the primary objective the international community should seek is to maintain the survival of the national system and national society itself.[3] In fact, the symbiotic relationship between nations and the international community can be traced back to Aristotle's theory on the relationship between man and the city-state that claims that man is an animal naturally inclined to city life because the self-sufficient city-state is the supreme-good social group naturally inclined to.[4] By contrast, the fundamental reason modern China is willing to fully participate in and actively maintain the stability of the international community is that China regards itself as a member of the international community, so that its own development can reach "perfection" only through relying on the stability and prosperity of the international community. Or, as the famous quote by the great American founding father Benjamin Franklin goes: "We must all hang together, or assuredly we shall all hang separately." Therefore, China has actively played a key role in many global issues concerning the survival of human community and has truly helped others overcome difficulties.

Third, China pursues an independent foreign policy of peace and is unwilling to be controlled by others. China does not seek hegemony, and neither will it be controlled by others. An important source for observing the behaviors of contemporary China is its modern history. From the First Opium War in 1839 to the founding of the People's Republic of China in 1949, China was constantly suffering from the pain of Western powers' invasions, which gives contemporary China a particular and much cherished complex of interdependence and autonomy. But one major consequence of the free ride is being led and intervened by the hegemonic power, to the detriment of national sovereignty. Therefore, China has clearly chosen a "strategic partnership" rather than "a free-ride strategy." The advantage of the former is that China can not only maintain independence but also cooperate with other countries to address common challenges. The core of the strategy lies in the "harmony but not sameness" in traditional Chinese values, yet the strategy can find resonance as well in social contract theory, which is of vital importance in Western culture and which claims that mutual respect, equal treatment, accepting conflicts, and peaceful coexistence are the connotations of a harmonious world. Therefore, the internal genes of Chinese culture once again indicate that China is unwilling to take the "free-ride" strategy.

It follows that whether from objective conditions or subjective desire, China is not a free rider in the international community but, rather, a country willing to make great contributions to building the international community based on giving consideration to both domestic development and foreign relations. Specific examples are the advocacy of fair reforms of the United Nations, meeting global challenges, carefully fulfilling treaty obligations, actively developing partnerships, and building regional cooperation mechanisms.

Actively Promoting Fair and Rational UN Reforms

The United Nations is the world's most authoritative intergovernmental organization. But as the international situation develops, the United Nations, which was born in the mid-twentieth century, is also facing the urgent task of constant reforms in order to adapt to the new international environment. As a founding member of the United Nations and a permanent member of the UN Security Council, China has made an important contribution to promoting the fair and rational reforms of the UN.

Back in September 1992, Chinese state councillor and foreign minister Qian Qichen comprehensively and systematically elaborated China's position on UN reforms for the first time when speaking at the forty-seventh General Assembly. In September 1994, Vice Premier and Foreign Minister Qian Qichen reemphasized when speaking at the forty-ninth General Assembly that "any reform of the United Nations should help maintain and enhance its current active role in international affairs and should help improve the efficiency of the United Nations; at the same time, the reforms should take into consideration the aspirations and interests of the vast majority of the developing countries and help them fully play their roles." In 1995, Chinese president Jiang Zemin further noted in his speech at the Special Commemorative Meeting for the 50th Anniversary of the United Nations that "We advocate carrying out necessary and appropriate reforms of the UN in a spirit of fairness, reason and full consultation and after serious deliberation and discussion."[5] In 2003, the United States bypassed the UN and launched a "preemptive" military attack on Iraq based on the excuse of "antiterrorism," thereby severely damaging the UN collective security mechanism. And a new round of reforms covering the authority of the UN was officially launched. To this end, UN secretary-general Kofi Annan put forward a formal reform text, but nations soon ran into huge differences. At this juncture, the Chinese Foreign Ministry issued on June 7 the Position Paper of the People's Republic of China on the United Nations Reforms, which clearly proposed five principles on UN reforms:

1. Reforms should be in the interest of multilateralism, and enhance UN's authority and efficiency, as well as its capacity to deal with new threats and challenges.
2. Reforms should safeguard the purposes and principles enshrined in the Charter of the United Nations, especially those of sovereign equality, non-interference in internal affairs, peaceful resolution of conflicts and strengthening international cooperation, etc.
3. Reforms should be all-dimensional and multisectoral, and aim to succeed in both aspects of security and development. Especially, reforms should aim at reversing the trend of "UN giving priority

to security over development" by increasing inputs in the field of development and facilitating the realization of the Millennium Development Goals.

4. Reforms shall accommodate the propositions and concerns of all UN members, especially those of the developing countries. Reforms should be based on democratic and thorough consultations and the most broadly based consensus.

5. Reforms should proceed gradually from tackling more manageable problems to thornier ones and be carried out in a way that will maintain and promote solidarity among members. For those proposals on which consensus has been reached, decision may be made promptly for their implementation; for important issues where division still exists, prudence, continued consultations and consensus-building are called for. It is undesirable to set a time limit or force a decision.[6]

On September 17, 2005, Chinese president Hu Jintao attended the United Nations sixtieth anniversary summit roundtable and made a speech entitled "Adhering to Democratic Consultation and Promoting Reforms," putting forward four proposals about the UN reforms, saying that members of the UN must:

1. Focus on the overall situation and adhere to the principles.
2. Promote democracy and have extensive consultations.
3. Have active reforms, steady and step by step.
4. Grasp the key points and comprehensively promote reforms.

It can be seen that the core of China's position on the UN reforms is trying to find a balance between efficiency and fairness that not only strengthens the role of the UN collective security mechanism in maintaining the stability of the international community but also ensures that the greatest possible number of countries can enjoy the UN's achievements in global governance. To this end, China has set an example as a responsible member of the UN Security Council by properly handling several important relations in the UN reforms:

- **First, the relationship between efficiency and fairness of the Security Council.** China is against the increase of vetoes in the Security Council, the purpose of which is to ensure the efficiency of its decision making. But China clearly advocates giving more countries, especially small countries, the opportunity to take turns to enter the UN Security Council and participate in the decision making.[7]

- **Second, the relationship between collective security and cooperative security.** China adheres to a new security concept of "mutual trust, mutual benefit, equality and cooperation" and advocates complementation between the formal UN collective security mechanism and flexible multilateral cooperative security so that each answers the purpose intended. China earnestly fulfills its responsibilities for collective security as a permanent member of the UN Security Council, actively participating in disarmament and peacekeeping operations. A typical example is that of the earthquake in Haiti in January 2010, when eight outstanding Chinese peacekeeping soldiers stuck to their posts and died in the line of duty, fully highlighting Chinese soldiers' courage and responsibility for peacekeeping missions. As an effective complement to the collective security mechanism, China also took the initiative to participate in actions maintaining regional security through multilateral cooperation, such as efforts to solve the DPRK nuclear issue and Iran nuclear issue and sending so far six groups of fleets to the Gulf of Aden in the Indian Ocean to cooperate with other countries in the combat against piracy.

- **Third, the relationship between the UN Security Council reforms and development.** China has always held that reforms should not only concern the Security Council but also focus on development issues and we should achieve the Millennium Development Goals as soon as possible, so that the developing countries can share the benefits of global governance by the UN. Therefore, the Chinese government has announced six initiatives for achieving the Millennium Development

Goals,[8] and set up the International Poverty Reduction Center in China in Beijing in May 2005. In March 2013, Chinese president Xi Jinping announced the Chinese government's new initiatives in supporting Africa at the dialogue meeting of BRICs and African leaders held in South Africa. The goals include establishing a multinational and multiregional infrastructure construction partnership to help Africa realize interconnection; carrying out consulting, planning, and feasibility studies and design of a resource center; and annually training 300 African management and technical staff members in the infrastructure sector. Another goal is to give priority to infrastructure implementation projects while making use of a US$20-billion credit supplied by China's government. Through investment and financial assistance, the president wants to encourage Chinese enterprises and financial institutions to get involved in cross-border multiregional African infrastructure and operational management.[9]

- **Fourth, the relationship between universality and particularity of human rights.** China has always attached importance to the human rights cause but believes that only under specific institutional arrangements based on different national conditions can universal human rights standards be achieved. At the same time China is firmly opposed to a few countries' seeking arrangements for political purposes under the pretext of human rights. To this end, China clearly emphasized the importance of avoiding the politicizing of work in the Human Rights Council so as to ensure countries' representation and to respect the diversity of the world before it voted in favor of establishment of the Human Rights Council in the UN General Assembly. China appreciates that the General Assembly mentioned several times in the preamble and operative paragraphs of its resolution a fair and nonselective approach to human rights issues in order to promote constructive dialogues and cooperation in the field of human rights, and China holds that this principle should be the guiding principle for the work of the council to avoid repeating the mistake of political confrontation in the Commission on Human Rights. Moreover, the Chinese government said that certain further concerns of China and some developing countries over human rights issues would be reflected in consultations after establishment of the Council.[10]

In September 2010, President Hu went to United Nations headquarters in New York to attend the summit on the Millennium Development Goals and again called for correct and reasonable reforms by the United Nations, believing that with joint efforts by China and the international community, United Nations reforms would achieve desired results. Moreover, the ultimate goal of UN reforms is to benefit human society. Therefore besides advocating reasonable reforms, China is shouldering the major responsibility of safeguarding the common interests of mankind in other areas, an outstanding action in response to the threat of global issues.

Coping with Common Challenges in Human Survival and Development

The emergence of global problems with wide coverage and intense penetrating power is a salient feature of changes in the post–Cold War international system. The global problems have a profound and far-reaching impact on human survival and development and therefore require close cooperation by all countries to jointly cope with them. As an emerging power, China is willing to fully integrate into the international community and naturally will not escape the responsibility of responding to common challenges faced by humankind, two of which are major threats: climate change and global epidemics.

Climate change has been one of the major international political issues since 2007, when the UN Intergovernmental Panel on Climate Change issued the fourth assessment report confirming that climate change resulted mainly from greenhouse gas emissions by human beings. In spite of doubts, extreme weather events that have occurred frequently in recent years indicate that the international community must take actions without delay to cope with climate changes. In this regard, China respects the scientific conclusion by the international experts and believes that climate change is a huge threat to human security, and therefore it is willing to participate in global governance of climate change. But China adheres to the principle of "common but differentiated responsibilities."

As a matter of fact, the root cause of increase in atmospheric temperature is industrial greenhouse gas emission by developed countries over the past centuries; the cumulative and per-capita emissions of developing countries are far below those of the developed ones. Therefore, it is the developed countries rather than developing countries that should bear the main responsibility of reducing greenhouse gas emission. Nevertheless, China remains an active partner in international cooperation to reduce emission and takes the initiative to reduce domestic greenhouse gas emission through completely transforming the mode of development. Although China is a non–Annex I country and does not need to set mandatory emission reduction targets according to the Kyoto Protocol, China still approved the Kyoto Protocol in 2002 and played an important role in promoting its entry into effect. Since then, China has actively participated in the Clean Development Mechanism (CDM) cooperation under the Kyoto Protocol, with its main indicators always ranking first (Tables 6.1, 6.2, and 6.3).

In terms of domestic emission reduction, from 1990 to 2007 global carbon dioxide emission per unit of output fell 15.4 percent, that of the United States decreased by 27 percent, developed countries' decreased by an average of 22 percent, developing countries an average of 10.2 percent, and China's 49.2 percent.[11] On this basis, the Chinese government proposed in November 2009 that by 2020 it would cut down carbon dioxide emission per unit of GDP by 40 to 45 percent from 2005. This demonstrates China's sense of responsibility in addressing climate change because this period of time coincides with the golden period of China's development, and arduous efforts are needed to achieve the goal.

Unlike the long-term threat posed by climate change, global epidemics are looming straight ahead. In the spring of 2003, the world was plagued by SARS (severe acute respiratory syndrome), and China,

Table 6.1 The Number and Proportion of Clean Development Projects Registered by Main Parties in the United Nations (by August 18, 2010, a total of 2,324)

Ranking	Party	Number of Projects Registered	Proportion (%)
1	China	923	39.72
2	India	520	22.38
3	Brazil	175	7.53
4	Mexico	123	5.29
5	Malaysia	83	3.57
6	Indonesia	48	2.07
7	Republic of Korea	43	1.85
8	Philippines	4	1.76

Source: http://cdm.unfccc.int/Statistics/Registration/NumOf RegisteredProjByHost PartiesPieChart.html.

Table 6.2 "Certified Emission Reduction" Issued by Main Hosts and Its Proportion (by August 18, 2010, a total of 428,605,720 tons)

Ranking	Party	"Certified Emission Reduction" (ton)	Proportion (%)
1	China	212,839,582	49.66
2	India	79,249,931	18.49
3	Republic of Korea	56,069,468	13.08
4	Brazil	42,188,444	9.84
5	Mexico	6,836,481	1.60

Source: http://cdm.unfccc.int/Statistics/Registration/NumOf RegisteredProjByHost PartiesPieChart.html.

as a member of the World Health Organization (WHO), played an important role in responding to the crisis. The Chinese government arranged a series of countermeasures to prevent the spread of the disease in time. Soon after the epidemic broke out, the CPC Central Committee Political Bureau Standing Committee held a meeting on

Table 6.3 Estimated "Certified Emission Reduction" and Proportion of Main Host Countries' CDM Projects

Ranking	Party	"Certified Emission Reduction" (ton)	Proportion (%)
1	China	229,523,057	60.75
2	India	43,154,160	11.42
3	Brazil	21,111,189	5.59
4	Republic of Korea	17,006,444	4.5
5	Mexico	9,597,832	2.54
6	Malaysia	5,097,247	1.35
7	Chile	4,711,692	1.25
8	Indonesia	4,326,425	1.15
9	Argentina	4,206,791	1.11
10	Nigeria	4,154,978	1.10

Source: http://cdm.unfccc.int/Statistics/Registration/NumOf RegisteredProjByHost PartiesPieChart.html.

April 17, 2003, discussed the issue of strengthening the prevention of SARS, required the establishment of a strict responsibility system, and forbade the delay of the report and the concealing of the epidemic. The following steps were then taken:

April 20: Regardless of losses in the tourism industry, China clearly stated that it supported the action of WHO naming Beijing and Shanxi as infected areas.

April 21: As requested by WHO, China began to announce the epidemic situation every day rather than once every five days previously.

April 25: China set up the national SARS Prevention and Control Headquarters and assigned Vice Premier Wu Yi as commander in chief and relevant ministers as team leaders so that the prevention of SARS was more institutionalized.

April 28: Premier Wen Jiabao went to Thailand to attend the China-ASEAN Leaders SARS Special Session. He stressed that the Chinese government was ready to face the difficulties and would, as always, deal with SARS with a responsible attitude, just as it had coped with the Asian financial crisis.

May 1: The world's largest epidemics hospital—the Beijing Xiaotangshan SARS Hospital—which was set up within only seven days and nights, formally received the first group of patients.

June 20: When the last group of patients were cured and left the hospital, they performed a high-speed operation of 51 days, with the world's lowest mortality rate, zero complaints, and zero infections of medical staff.[12] At the same time, Chinese scientists' close cooperation with foreign counterparts played a key role in developing the SARS vaccine.

On March 19, 2003, when the epidemic reached its peak, Wuhan University in China announced that the results of joint research conducted by the School of Life Sciences of Wuhan University, New York Blood Center, and Mount Sinai School of Medicine had explained the fusion mechanism of SARS virus and found the peptide inhibitor against SARS virus.

In the spring of 2009, the globe was plagued by Influenza H1N1 that began in Mexico and the United States. China once again demonstrated an image of a responsible power. Based on the experience of coping with SARS, the Chinese government had arranged preventive measures before cases were found in China, and information disclosure was conducted in a more timely manner. For example, after the first suspected case emerged in Sichuan, in order to avoid the spread of panic and suspicion, the Chengdu municipal government held a press conference at 3 a.m. on May 11, 2009, playing an important role in preventing and controlling the spread of the epidemic. Meanwhile, China maintained good communication with the World Health Organization. For example, on May 13, Chinese health minister Chen Zhu had a talk with WHO director general Margaret Chan on the phone, exchanging views on the Influenza H1N1 prevention and control strategies, the characteristics and development of this epidemic, and the development and storage of antiviral drugs and vaccine.[13]

In terms of vaccine development, under the multisector unified leadership of a vaccine R&D and joint production coordination mechanism, China carried out the world's largest vaccine clinical trials in seven provinces (on more than 13,000 people). The results showed that the inoculation of one dose of 15µg of Influenza H1N1 virus split vaccine could prevent the virus effectively, with a protection rate of over 85 percent. What was particularly important was that the vaccine was highly safe, with an adverse reaction rate no higher than that of seasonal influenza vaccines and no serious adverse reactions. The results of clinical trials in some other countries also supported the conclusion of clinical trials in China. In early September, approved by the China Food and Drug Administration, Influenza H1N1 vaccine was put into production. China became the world's first country that had completed vaccine development and registered use. The remarkable achievement received recognition by WHO, and some countries showed the intention of purchasing the vaccine from China.[14] In addition, China offered assistance to other countries. For example, China offered US$1 million convertible foreign exchange and US$4 million worth of supplies to Mexico to fight against the epidemic in April 2009, when the epidemic was most serious.

Facts have proved that in the face of global challenges, China has always connected its own destiny with the fate of the human community and exerted itself to bear the international responsibility of coping with challenges. On the other hand, the transnational nature of global challenges also requires countries to continue to strengthen domestic governance capacity, so China is earnestly fulfilling relevant treaty obligations while strengthening international cooperation to deal with common threats.

Conscientiously Fulfilling Treaty Obligations

Conscientiously fulfilling treaty obligations is not only an important manifestation of a country shouldering international responsibilities but also an effective way to boost a country's own modernization through learning international norms. With this dual role in mind, China has made outstanding achievements in fulfilling international treaty obligations. So far, China has joined more than 100 intergovernmental organizations and signed nearly 300 multilateral international treaties.[15]

China acceded to the Biological Weapons Convention (BWC) in 1984 and has consistently supported and actively participated in multilateral efforts aimed at strengthening the effectiveness of the convention. China has actively participated in the BWC Review Conference and submitted a report on obligation fulfillment. Since 1988, China has submitted BWC confidence-building announcement data to the United Nations every year, according to the decisions of the Review Conference. China also actively participated in the negotiations on the BWC protocol and the annual meetings of convention parties and meetings of the expert panel.

China also actively participated in the negotiations of the Chemical Weapons Convention (CWC) and strongly advocated bringing prohibition of the use of chemical weapons and proper disposal of abandoned chemical weapons into the scope of the convention and eventually making the convention a truly comprehensive international legal instrument on the prohibition of chemical weapons.

As an original convention party, China has made positive contributions to effectively fulfilling the CWC and promoting its universality. China has established and continuously improved its domestic legal system and measures and strengthened the capacity of national institutions to facilitate fulfillment of the obligations. According to CWC requirements and national conditions, China has established obligation fulfillment institutions at both the central and local levels, forming an obligation fulfillment system of effective management covering the whole country. In some areas of developed chemical industry, obligation fulfillment institutions at city and county levels have been established. China has also submitted its initial declaration and all the annual declarations on time and completely, according to the provisions of the convention. By the end of June 2005, China had received 95 on-site inspections by the Organisation for the Prohibition of Chemical Weapons, and all the results demonstrated that China had strictly implemented its obligations to the convention.

The Chinese government has also continued to promote implementation of the CWC in Hong Kong and Macau Special Administrative Region. In 2004, the Hong Kong Special Administrative Region completed obligation fulfillment legislation. The government submitted its declaration through the central government and started fulfilling its obligations. Preparatory work of obligation fulfillment including legislation in Macau is being carried out smoothly. The Chinese government also pays attention to implementation of the CWC in Taiwan and will continue to seek a proper solution to this problem under the premise of one China.[16]

Since its accession to the Protocol on Prohibitions or Restrictions on the Use of Mines, Body-Trap and Other Devices, China has actively fulfilled its obligations. From 2006 to 2007, more than 50 tons of old antipersonnel landmines (APLs) and other explosives that do not meet the provisions of the protocol and do not have transformation value were destroyed. The Chinese military has set up eight professional agencies responsible for detecting and destroying old mines and blasting equipment. In addition, the Chinese military has set up a number of mine technology laboratories in Beijing, Shenyang, Nanjing, and other cities, carrying out case studies such as mine detectability, self-destruction technology, and mine destruction techniques and achieved positive results. The Chinese military has carried out the technological transformation of APLs that do not meet the requirements of the technical appendix of the protocol and has made progress in new alternative weapons development. Meanwhile, the Chinese Ministry of National Defense has coproduced a publicity and educational film, *Mine Obligation Fulfillment Knowledge*, with Chinese TV stations and broadcast the film in China. The film has also been recorded on CD-ROM to be distributed to engineering troops and has obtained favorable results. The Chinese Foreign Ministry and Ministry of National Defense have carried out publicity and training activities on mine obligation fulfillment in the army, airborne troops, and marines, propagating knowledge on mine obligation fulfillment and further enhancing the awareness of using mines according to the law.

In addition, China continues to support and participate in the humanitarian de-mining process in African countries. China has held de-mining trainings of one and a half months for Angola, Burundi, Chad, Guinea Bissau, and Mozambique within the framework of the China-Africa Cooperation Forum and provided free of charge an amount of humanitarian de-mining equipment. Meanwhile, Chinese peacekeeping sapper units sent to Lebanon actively participated in the de-mining action in Lebanon and received certification by the United Nations De-mining Action Coordination Center in Lebanon with a total clearance of over 10,000 mines and unexploded ordnance, playing an important role in the peacekeeping de-mining actions in Lebanon.[17]

As a member of the World Trade Organization, China made a lot of solemn commitments when acceding to the WTO, such as reducing tariffs on 5,000 commodities, canceling nontariff restrictions on over 100 kinds of goods, unifying the foreign exchange market, and substantially reducing tariffs on more than 2,000 kinds of textiles and chemical products—in eight years since 1997 gradually abolishing import quotas of cars, small buses, and automotive parts, in six years since 1997 removing import quotas of motorcycles, cameras, and compressors, upon accession to the WTO abolishing 66 import quotas of sugar, cigars, and certain woolen and cotton products, increasing the amount while gradually abolishing the quotas, not introducing agricultural subsidies upon accession to the WTO and reducing the average tariff to 10 percent in 2005, and so on.[18] In addition, China made another promise of protecting intellectual property rights from the date of accession to the WTO onward, according to the Agreement on Trade-Related Aspects of Intellectual Property Rights (TRIPs), and has made important achievements in this regard (Figure 6.5).

In 2009, local intellectual property rights (IPR) administrations across the country received and handled a total of 937 patent violation dispute cases and 26 cases of other types of disputes. Thirty cases involving fraudulent use of others' patents and 548 cases regarding

Figure 6.5 The Growth Trend of the Number of Pirated Products Searched and Confiscated by the Chinese Government (1998–2005)

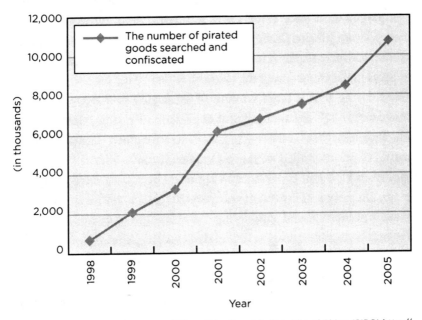

Source: State Intellectual Property Office of the People's Republic of China (SIPO),http://www.nipso.cn/bai.asp#.

counterfeiting patents were investigated and dealt with. In 2009, the Administration for Industry and Commerce (AIC) at all levels across China investigated 51,044 cases of violations concerning trademarks, among which 7,448 were general violations, and 43,596 were related to trademark infringement and counterfeiting; 10,461 foreign-related trademark cases were investigated and handled. The AIC seized and removed 13.534 million illegal trademark labels and handed over 92 cases and 109 suspects to judicial authorities for suspected criminal violations concerning trademark.

In 2009, the customs across the country took IPR protection measures a total of 67,051 times and actually detained 65,810 batches of cargo suspicious of infringement, increased by 4.1 times and 4.9 times, respectively, compared with those in 2008, with actual detainment of 280 million items of goods worth of a total value of 450 million RMB.

Under the unified arrangement by the General Administration of Customs (GAC), the customs nationwide carried out special enforcement campaigns with clear targets and improved their enforcement efficiency. From June to December 2009, GAC initiated a special IPR protection campaign against infringement activities through a mailing and express mail system across the country, which lasted for seven months. Considering that a large volume of infringing goods are exported abroad through the mailing and express mail system, the supervising authorities took effective measures to strengthen the actual monitoring of goods mailed or express mailed abroad—especially of those mailed to high-risk countries and regions—by raising their inspection ratio, realizing a 100-percent-computerized machine check when conditions permitted, and simplifying the procedure of detaining infringing mailbags and express mail and their investigation and prosecution process. During the period of the special campaign, customs across China seized 37,918 batches of infringing goods, with a total value of 61,662,700 RMB and 2,612,900 items involved, through the mailing and express mail system.[19]

As a non–Annex I member of the United Nations Framework Convention on Climate Change, China not only carefully inventoried greenhouse gas emissions according to the regulations, timely submitted national information notification, and actively carried out public education but also voluntarily introduced significant system reforms, the most prominent example of which is the Renewable Energy Law of the People's Republic of China, which came into effect on January 1, 2006, making China one of the world's few countries legislating for renewable energy. At present, the law is under further modification and improvement. In terms of institution building, the State Council established in June 2007 a leading group in response to climate change and energy saving and emission reduction, with Premier Wen as head and including top leaders of 29 ministries, aimed at enhancing inter-departmental coordination, integrating resources, and improving the efficiency of response. This was followed by the upgrade of the State Environmental Protection Administration to the Ministry of Environmental Protection, described as the "highlight of the highlights" of the year's ministerial reform by the French European Times, demonstrating that "the Chinese government has lifted environmental protection to the same important level as industry, agriculture, transportation, energy and other departments, making it one of the vital industries concerning the national economic lifeline."[20]

In addition, China has made significant progress in fulfilling obligations of treaties concerning social development and environmental protection such as the International Covenant on Economic, Social and Cultural Rights, the International Covenant on Civil and Political Rights, and the Montreal Protocol on Substances That Deplete the Ozone Layer and has strived for harmony together with other members of the international community through actively developing partnerships with the treaties as a link.

Actively Developing Partnership Relations

The mode of relations between nations reflects the basic judgments of countries about the nature of the international system. China believes that the theme of the present era is peace and development. On one hand, a world war is unlikely to break out in the foreseeable future, with the declining role of military factors; on the other hand, various types of countries have the need for development and therefore must seek cooperation. Coincidentally, American scholars Robert Keohane and Joseph Nye have put forward a similar theory that relations among countries have entered an era of complex interdependence, characterized by the use of multiple channels in international communications, the absence of a hierarchy of issues on the agenda of interstate relationship, and a decline in the use of military force and coercive power.[21] This shows that people of insight in China and in the Western world have all recognized major changes in the contemporary international system and that countries need to adopt a new mode of communications. And China has chosen the mode of partnership.

Different from the military character of alliance and the inequality of hegemony, partnership is based on mutual respect and equal treatment and is not against any third party, meaning that China will conduct relations with all countries, big or small, strong or weak, on the basis of the Five Principles of Peaceful Coexistence. Therefore, China has partnerships around the world. The means of partnerships is cooperation—that is, to seek common development, work together to address crises, and properly handle differences through various channels. Therefore, one major feature of China's partnerships is to continuously establish and improve various cooperative mechanisms. The purpose of partnerships is to abandon ideological confrontations and focus on pragmatic cooperation. Therefore, China's partnerships exist in various forms and achieve remarkable results.

Specifically, the China-Russia strategic partnership of cooperation is a typical partnership between neighboring powers. The two countries not only actively developed economic and trade relations—with bilateral trade volume increased by nearly twofold in five years and China becoming Russia's fourth-largest trading partner, ranking first among Asia-Pacific Economic Cooperation (APEC) members—but also completely resolved the border issue left over by history through equal consultations in 2008, laying the foundation for further development of the partnership. In addition, China and Russia have effectively deterred regional terrorism, ethnic separatism, and religious extremism through several joint military exercises and have closely cooperated in multilateral mechanisms to address crises such as the DPRK nuclear issue and the Iran nuclear issue, playing an important role in international and regional stability.

The China-DPRK good-neighborly and friendly cooperative relation is a typical partnership between two countries with the same type of state system. The two countries are not fettered by the same ideology but, rather, focus on pragmatic cooperation based on national interests. For example, to assist in economic development in the DPRK, Chinese premier Wen signed practical documents such as the Agreement on Joint Construction, Management and Maintenance of the Yalu River Highway Bridge and the Memorandum of Understanding on Detailed Implementation Plans of Chinese Tourist Groups Traveling in the DPRK. The two countries have also reached important consensus on promoting the denuclearization of the Korean Peninsula and maintained the mechanism of six-party talks, easing tension on the peninsula.

China-Japan strategic relations of mutual benefit is a typical partnership between two countries with historical grievances. The two countries are, first, close economic and trade partners: China surpassed the United States to become Japan's largest export market when bilateral trade volume reached US$266.79 billion in 2008; Japan is the second-largest foreign investor in China. Meanwhile, the two countries have made efforts to properly handle differences. For example, in November 2006, the two countries' foreign ministers reached a consensus on the common research on history and agreed that China and Japan would each set up a committee of 10 scholars, consisting of two groups of "ancient history" and "modern history," and the two sides would take turns hosting the meetings. The committee issued the Chinese and Japanese versions of the common research report on history, reaching a consensus on such issues as the aggressive nature of the China-Japan War and the death toll of the Nanjing Massacre. On the issue of East China Sea, the two countries reached an agreement in principle in June 2008 and designated seven specific areas for common development. In addition, the two countries have conducted equal consultations on such issues as the Diaoyu Islands, the Taiwan issue, food security, and regional security while actively developing growth points of bilateral cooperation in environmental protection and new energy, maintaining a strategic relation of mutual benefit and regional stability.

China–European Union (EU) comprehensive strategic partnership is a typical North-South partnership. Despite different developmental levels, histories, cultures, and values, bilateral economic and trade relations have developed rapidly in a stable political framework. The EU is China's largest trading partner and largest source of technological imports. China is the EU's largest source of imports and the second-largest trading partner. On this basis, China and the EU take advantage of various mechanisms to properly handle differences. For example, by June 2010, the two sides had held 29 human rights dialogues, and in the most recent one, the EU made positive comments on

China's achievements in human rights. In addition, both China and the EU advocate multilateralism in international affairs and cooperate closely in response to global challenges. For example, in April 2010, the two sides issued the Joint Statement on Dialogue and Cooperation on Climate Change; announced the establishment of ministerial dialogue and a cooperation mechanism on climate change, as well as a ministerial hotline on climate change; and launched the China-EU Clean Energy Center in Beijing. In other words, there are not only traditional North-South supply and demand relations between China and the EU but also high-technology research and development cooperation. Another typical example is the Galileo satellite navigation technology cooperation and the international thermonuclear reactor cooperation in France. This is undoubtedly a model of partnership between the North and the South.

China-Africa's new strategic partnership is a typical South-South partnership. China-Africa relations have a long history. After establishment of the People's Republic of China, the two sides established a deep friendship based on common historical experiences and the needs for development. In the new century, China has continued its traditional friendship with Africa and at the same time brought new content into their relations, which is mainly reflected in improving the developmental capacities of African counties. For instance, by the end of 2012, China had been providing assistance for 53 African countries (as of 2013, 49 African countries maintain normal diplomatic relations with China). More than 1,000 complete sets of projects have been constructed involving agriculture and industry, infrastructure, public buildings, culture, education, health, and other fields; more than 350,000 technical personnel have been dispatched to Africa for help; more than 53,700 African talents have been trained in China; and 42 medical teams have been dispatched to African countries, with 397 youth volunteers dispatched to 15 countries, including Ethiopia and Seychelles. At the same time, China has also been providing production and living supplies, technical assistance and cash assistance for a large number of recipients who are in urgent need. This shows that the China-Africa partnership is not "new colonialism" but, rather, sincere friendship withstanding the test of time.

Although China and Brazil are far apart geographically, their partnership is representative of partnership between emerging countries. In 1993, Brazil became the first developing country to have a strategic partnership with China, and since then, the two countries have had pragmatic cooperation in various fields. In November 2004, President Hu went to Brazil on a state visit, initiating a new era of bilateral relations. China is now Brazil's largest trading partner, largest export destination, and second-largest source of imports. In May 2009, Brazil set up its largest overseas trade representative office in Beijing. Climate change is a new field in the China-Brazil partnership. Brazil has new energy technology advantages and China has a huge market, providing favorable conditions for the two countries to expand cooperation. In addition, the two sides have also had close cooperation with India and South Africa under the United Nations Framework Convention on Climate Change forming BASIC countries, successfully defending the basic framework of the international climate mechanism.

China and the United States are the world's largest developing and developed countries, and whose bilateral relations are of global significance. The two sides are committed to strengthening comprehensive cooperation to jointly address challenges and have achieved initial results in response to climate change, financial crises, and nonproliferation. For instance, in order to reduce greenhouse gas emissions, the China-U.S. Clean Energy Research Center was established in July 2009. Under that multilateral consultation mechanism, the two sides have worked together with relevant countries to respond to the financial crisis and ease the nuclear proliferation crises on the Korean Peninsula and in the Middle East. Despite ups and downs, the China-U.S. partnership will finally be established and improved as long as the two sides adhere to the principle of mutual respect, equality, and mutual benefit.

Constructing Regional Cooperation Regimes

Regional cooperation is a major trend of international relations today, the core of which is regime building. The main function of international regimes is to facilitate the formation of specific

intergovernmental cooperative agreements,[22] provide a stable platform for communications, facilitate exchanges of information, reduce
erroneous judgments, and regulate behaviors. China's contribution
to promoting regional cooperation through regime building is mainly
reflected in the East Asian and the Asia Pacific regions.

The East Asian economies began to boom after the wave of globalization in the 1960s. However, defects in the development mode
appeared in the late 1990s and finally led to a severe financial crisis in 1997. At that time, China was at a crucial point of transition
to a market economy and needed stable export growth as a guarantee. But considering the spreading effect of the crisis, China insisted on
not devaluing the RMB, providing a broad export market for other
East Asian countries. That responsible behavior as a big power won
wide acclaim from the international community and alleviated East
Asian countries' political misgivings about China, marking the pre-
lude to China's continuous efforts to build the regional cooperation
mechanism.

On December 16, 1997, the first ASEAN-China Leaders Meeting was held in Kuala Lumpur. Then Chinese president Jiang Zemin
attended the meeting and delivered an important speech entitled
"Establishing a Good-Neighborly Partnership of Mutual Trust Orien-
tated toward the Twenty-first Century." The meeting issued the "Joint
Statement of the Meeting of Heads of State/Government of the Member States of ASEAN and the President of the People's Republic of
China," establishing the China-ASEAN good-neighborly partnership
of mutual trust toward the twenty-first century. Since then, "ASEAN-
China" (10+1) Leaders Meetings have been held annually. At the
sixth meeting, on November 4, 2002, the two sides signed the Framework Agreement on Comprehensive Economic Cooperation between
ASEAN and the People's Republic of China and agreed to build the
China-ASEAN Free Trade Area (CAFTA) in 2010.

In January 2010, the free-trade area covering 1.9 billion people,
with a GDP of nearly US$6 trillion and a trade volume of US$4.5 trillion, was officially launched, with over 7,000 kinds of goods traded
at zero tariff. In the six months after CAFTA was launched, bilateral

trade between China and ASEAN totaled US$136.49 billion, up by 54.7 percent. China's export to ASEAN was US$64.6 billion, up by 45.4 percent, and import from ASEAN was US$71.89 billion, up by 64 percent. At present, ASEAN has surpassed Japan to become China's third-largest trading partner. From 2003 to 2008, China's direct investment in ASEAN increased from US$230 million to US$2.18 billion, with an increase of nearly nine times. By April 2010, total two-way investments between China and ASEAN had reached about US$70 billion, of which China's investments in ASEAN totaled about US$10 billion. In addition, to ensure smooth operation of the cooperation mechanism, China arranged a 20-day CAFTA seminar for ASEAN officials in charge of economy and trade. Facts have proved that despite the huge difference between the sizes of the countries, both China and ASEAN have enjoyed the practical benefits brought by the bilateral economic cooperation mechanism based on the principle of equality and mutual benefit and have made the mechanism a new model of South-South cooperation.[23]

In addition, China and ASEAN issued the Joint Declaration of ASEAN and China on Cooperation in the Field of Non-Traditional Security Issues at the sixth ASEAN-China Leaders Meeting. Foreign ministers and representatives of foreign ministers of China and members of ASEAN also signed the Declaration on the Conduct of Parties in the South China Sea, confirming that China and ASEAN are committed to strengthening their good-neighborly partnership of mutual trust, jointly safeguarding peace and stability in the South China Sea region, and emphasizing resolution of disputes about the South China Sea through friendly consultations, negotiations, and peaceful means. This is an institutional guarantee for safeguarding regional security in the South China Sea.

On October 8, 2003, Premier Wen attended the seventh ASEAN-China Leaders Meeting and delivered a speech with "Comprehensive and Thorough Cooperation and Promotion of Peace and Prosperity" as the theme. Meanwhile, the Chinese government announced its accession to the Treaty of Amity and Cooperation in Southeast Asia and signed the Joint Declaration of ASEAN and China on Strategic

Partnership for Peace and Prosperity, establishing the China-ASEAN strategic partnership and providing a new political guarantee for the bilateral cooperation mechanism.

In the framework of the ASEAN 10+3, China, Japan, and the Republic of Korea established a regular meeting mechanism between the leaders in 1999, the content of which covers major strategic issues among the three countries about regional and global economy and trade, security, culture, and environment. After that, under China's active promotion, the three countries in December 2008 officially launched a regular meeting mechanism between leaders independent of the 10+3 framework and issued the Joint Statement on Tripartite Partnership at the first meeting, clearly setting the orientation of the tripartite partnership and its direction and principles of cooperation. The meeting also issued practical documents such as the Joint Statement on International Financial and Economic Issues, the Joint Statement on Disaster Management, and the Action Plan for Promoting Tripartite Cooperation. The second summit of leaders was held in Beijing in 2009 and issued the Joint Statement of the Tenth Anniversary of Trilateral Cooperation and the Joint Declaration on Sustainable Development and agreed on 10 cooperation initiatives. The third summit, held in the Republic of Korea at the end of May 2010, coincided with the *Cheonan* incident and the deterioration of relations between the DPRK and the Republic of Korea. Under China's active coordination, the meeting concluded that the three countries should "maintain communication and properly handle this incident to maintain regional peace and stability."

At the same time, China has focused on building wider Asia-Pacific cooperation mechanisms in an open and cooperative spirit. For example, in order to promote economic and technological cooperation in the region, China proposed at the fourth APEC leaders informal meeting in 1996 the establishment of a network of APEC science and technology industrial parks and promised to open several of China's own national science and technology industrial parks for APEC members. At the sixth leaders informal meeting in 1998, a previous proposal by China—formulating a "Cooperation Agenda for Science and Technology Industry toward the Twenty-first Century"—was implemented. In addition, China also announced at this meeting that it would provide US$10 million to set up a "China APEC Science and Technology Industry Cooperation Fund." In November 2009, the Chinese government once again announced the allocation of US$10 million to set up the China APEC Cooperation Fund to encourage and support relevant Chinese authorities and enterprises in their participation in economic and technological cooperation in APEC.

To conclude, the East Asian and Asia-Pacific region is the primary economic partner and security barrier for China's peaceful development. Such development will bring a rare opportunity for the overall development of this region. Therefore, China has always held an open attitude to actively promote the building of cooperation mechanisms in the East Asian and Asia-Pacific region and advocates integration and complementation of multiple mechanisms. Under the joint efforts of China and other countries in this region, the East Asian and Asia-Pacific region has become one of the most active regions in economic and social development in today's world, which fully reflects China's responsibility of promoting regional stability and development as a big power.

Case Study—China's Role and Responsibility in Governance of Climate Change

The international community generally expects China to take the lead in responding to the threat of climate change in accordance with its growing strength, while China's primary task at present is domestic development. According to the principle of reciprocity of "rights, responsibilities, and interests," China's participation in governance of climate change should not undermine its sovereignty. Therefore, how to reach a balance and reconcile domestic and international development is crucial in undertaking international responsibilities on climate change. Currently, China has taken many substantive steps.

First, China has made clear changes in domestic policies in order to reduce its own greenhouse gas emissions. The Chinese government wrote into its 11th Five-Year Plan for the first time a cumulative reduction in energy consumption per unit GDP of 20 percent in five years and other binding targets, though the primary task during the financial crisis is to stimulate economic growth. Even in times of crisis, the Ministry of Environmental Protection still complied with strict rules.[24] Consequently, by February 2009, when the crisis was most serious, 14 of the 194 projects submitted to the Ministry of Environmental Protection had been suspended or disproved. In addition, President Hu said when he attended the 2009 China International Energy-Saving and New Energy Technologies Expo that "in the current situation of international financial crisis, energy conservation and emission reduction and new energy development should be emphasized."[25] Following this request, not a penny of the 4-trillion-RMB financial stimulus package entered the high-pollution, high-energy-consumption, and resource-demanding industries. Instead, 44 percent of the package was spent on livelihood projects; 16 percent on independent innovations, restructuring, energy conservation, emission reduction, and ecological development; 23 percent on major infrastructure construction; 14 percent on Wenchuan earthquake reconstruction; and 3 percent on other public spending.[26]

The Chinese government has made another important policy change in order to address climate change, which is to establish the "energy-saving and environmentally friendly society pilot area" based on the sustainable development pilot area. On December 24, 2007, soon after the Conference of the Parties of the United Nations Framework Convention on Climate Change in Bali, Indonesia, the Chinese government approved the development of the Wuhan City Circle and three cities in Hunan—namely, Changsha, Zhuzhou, and Xiangtan— into the country's energy-saving and environmentally friendly pilot areas of comprehensive coordinated reform on social construction, aiming at "effectively taking a new way different from the traditional model of urbanization and industrialization, and playing an exemplary and leading role in promoting national institutional reforms and achieving scientific development and social harmony."[27]

China set up a number of pilot areas for sustainable development at the beginning of the reform and opening up, which is to give policy support to certain counties and cities for the implementation of sustainable development experiments. But they were of small scale, constituting only 31 percent of the urban areas of big cities—that is, to set up pilot areas in certain areas of big cities, such as Jiang'an District of Wuhan.[28] However, the energy-saving and environmentally friendly society pilot area in Wuhan City Circle includes eight large and medium-size cities surrounding Wuhan, accounting for 33 percent of the area in Hubei province, its GDP and financial revenue in 2004 accounting for 73 percent and 74 percent of the province, respectively. Changsha, Zhuzhou, and Xiangtan Urban Agglomeration account for 13.3 percent of the total area of Hunan province, the population, GDP, and financial revenue accounting for 19.2 percent, 37.6 percent, and 38.2 percent of the province, respectively. More important, the steel, automobile, machinery, high-technology, metallurgy, pharmaceutical, chemical, and power industries are concentrated in the two pilot areas, making them important industrial areas as well as major energy consuming centers. Therefore, they are of unsurpassable strategic significance for China to explore a new way different from the traditional model of urbanization and industrialization.

These changes show that China has entered a new era of economic growth optimized by environmental protection from an old one of economic growth at the expense of environmental deterioration,[29] seeking to make achievements in both development and environmental protection through completely changing the way of development and bringing about significant results. By the end of 2009, China had eliminated 1.1 billion tons of carbon dioxide emissions through energy saving and consumption reduction. At present, more than 2,000 energy-saving and emission-reducing projects are in the application and approval stage in China. If all got implemented, they were expected to eliminate 2.2 billion tons of carbon dioxide emissions by 2012. On this basis, China is considering setting some "green index" such as "renewable and clean energy consumption ratio" and "carbon dioxide emission reduced per unit GDP" in its 12th Five-Year Plan to evaluate local officials' performance.[30] In April 2010, a research conducted by the United Nations Environment Programme and independent nonprofit institutions showed that 46 percent of countries had made progress in climate accountability since the Copenhagen Summit, and among them, Germany, China, and the Republic of Korea did the best.[31]

China also has played a key role in promoting the building of the international climate regime. China is a key force in maintaining and innovating existing basic principles of an international climate regime. The international climate regime—with the United Nations Framework Convention on Climate Change, the Kyoto Protocol, and their follow-up documents as the main content—is the institutional guarantee for current global governance of climate change—the basic principle of which is that the parties shall undertake "common but differentiated responsibilities." However, developed countries generally want to abolish the Kyoto Protocol and reinvent the wheel. The cost of establishing a new regime is obviously higher than the cost of maintaining the existing one, which requires a strong political will to maintain the existing regime so as to continue the negotiations on the basis of the results achieved. China has made contributions in this regard.

As Premier Wen pointed out at the Copenhagen Summit: "The United Nations Framework Convention on Climate Change and the Kyoto Protocol are achievements through countries' long and hard work and are the combination of a broad consensus. They are the legal basis and guide for international cooperation on climate change and should be cherished and developed. The results of this meeting must uphold rather than obscure the basic principles of the Convention and its protocol; must follow and not deviate from the 'Bali Roadmap' license; must focus on and not deny consensus reached and progress in the negotiations."[32] It is with the support of firm political will that China promoted the agreement in the Copenhagen Accord, laying the foundation for climate negotiations in Cancún, Mexico, in 2010.

In addition, if China could successfully achieve the carbon intensity emission reduction targets set up for itself, it would surely strengthen the norm of the Kyoto Protocol calling for a voluntary emission reduction in developing countries and set an example for the international community. To achieve this goal, though China was opposed to the principle of "subject to domestic measurement, reporting, and verification," it still agreed with the Copenhagen Accord that the result would be reported through national communications every two years with provisions for international consultations and analysis under clearly defined guidelines.[33] On the other hand, as for the problem of responsibility determination concerning the Kyoto Protocol, the Chinese government has always stressed the impartiality of per-capita carbon emissions measurement. If this principle is to be written into a new global climate agreement, it would undoubtedly be a major innovative contribution to construction of the international climate regime.[34]

Second, China is a key force in promoting the transfer of global new energy technologies. Developed countries' reluctance regarding government-led transfer of low-carbon technologies to developing countries is one of the core problems hindering the development of the international climate regime. Chinese scholars say a feasible solution is the establishment of specialized institutions and mechanisms for inter-governmental cooperation for transfer of technology and funds.[35] It is the insistence of developing countries represented by China that all parties eventually compromise to add the establishment of a "Copenhagen Green Climate Fund" into the Copenhagen Accord as a main body for improving developing countries' mitigation and adaptation and the transfer of capital and technologies. Although specific institutional arrangements need to be further negotiated, this expression means that countries have taken the first step toward the government-led technological transfer.

Third, China is a key force in achieving regional governance of climate change. One problem in current global governance of climate change is that too many countries are involved in a single agreement, so the coordination of interests is extremely difficult. Therefore, the reasonable arrangements of international climate mechanisms should be based on a package of agreements among countries, groups of countries, and regions. An approach based on agreements or partnerships between individual nations, groups of countries, and regions makes more sense and could eventually act to strengthen more universal measures.[36] At present, a successful example of regional climate governance is the European Union, whereas the climate governance in the Asia-Pacific region has achieved remarkable results under China's active promotion.

China has actively participated in multilateral energy cooperation and made efforts to implement energy initiatives since it became a member of the APEC. It has made outstanding achievements in effectively promoting cooperation in energy efficiency and energy conservation, new energy and renewable energy, and energy transport and infrastructure.[37] President Hu proposed at the fifteenth APEC Informal Leaders' Meeting in 2007 the establishment of "the network of Asia-Pacific forest rehabilitation and sustainable management" aiming at promoting the recovery and sustainable management of forests in the Asia-Pacific region through information sharing, policy dialogue, capacity-building and demonstration projects, enhancement of the productive capacity and ecological functions of forest ecosystems, and giving full play to forests in mitigating climate change. The objectives are to promote recovery of regional forests and to carry out afforestation and reforestation, contributing to the objective of "growth of 20 million hectares of all kinds of forests in APEC region before 2020."[38] The network was officially launched in September 2008 in Beijing, providing a new platform and opportunities for climate governance in the Asia-Pacific region. A major advantage of climate governance in the Asia-Pacific region is that the world's major greenhouse gas emitters are concentrated in this region, and a variety of mechanisms for cooperation coexist, convenient for not only a combination of many small-scale *climate* governances but also *effective* governance. As an important member of many international mechanisms in the Asia-Pacific region, China will undoubtedly be a key force in driving regional climate governance.

Fourth, China is a key force in assisting developing countries in their responses to climate changes. From 2000 to 2009, China held 50 energy-saving- and environmental-protection-training classes for developing countries, including hydropower, methane, and other renewable-energy-training classes. Meanwhile, China also offered direct renewable energy assistance to developing countries to enhance their abilities to respond to climate changes. For instance, China built solar photovoltaic equipment for Cuba in April 2005, the annual production capacity of which is 200-peak kilowatt. China helped build an ecological demonstration farm with a methane system for Tonga in December 2009. In addition, China took the initiative to help small island countries alleviate direct threats brought about by climate changes. For example, China started construction of the safe-island project, which moved residents from lowlands to highlands in October 2009 in Maldives, including 47 one-floor residential units covering a total of 4,447 square meters. These initiatives have played a positive role in helping developing countries mitigate and adapt to the threats of climate changes.

Despite great pressure, the Chinese government is still trying to reach a balance between domestic development and responding to climate change, highlighting China's remarkable sense of responsibility for the building of international community and the maintenance of common human security.

CHAPTER 7

THE
"CHINA GOSPEL"
THEORY

Compared with various theories concerning China, the "China Gospel" theory may be an appropriate account for China's global influence and its international responsibilities. In the economic respect, a rising China provides unprecedented opportunities and driving forces for global development. Various countries and regions will benefit from the economic development in China. Chinese products of great quality but lower price enhance the living standard and well-being throughout the whole world so, how significantly would people be affected without Chinese products? China's constant demands for resources and commodities alter the subordinate status of primary products in the global economic and trade structure, benefiting the financial conditions and foreign exchange earnings of many countries. Also, China provides an enormous market for investors to realize their "China dream." Furthermore, China's aid to developing countries draws the attention of developed countries and also emerging countries such as Russia and India to the developing countries, accelerating development there.

In the political respect, a rising China can balance the distribution of power in the world, breaking the 500-year structure of Western-centrism. Since modern times, the West has established its central status in the contemporary international system through institutional reforms, commercial expansions, and military conquest. Despite numerous conflicts and wars, the West remains dominant in power structure, agenda setting, and values.[1] China actively engages itself in the existing international system and will not resort to extremist measures to overthrow the international political and economic orders. But objectively, a rising China will be helpful to promote political multipolarization and democratization. The development of China is significant to reform the irrational international order and achieve fair distribution of global resources. Due to the rise of China, the Western world may not be able to depend on poorer countries and the future of their posterity to have further development. Instead, they have to face the challenges brought by their economic and social system and reconsider the need for reforms and renovations—and stimulation of the driving force for social development. China's development motivates Western countries to readjust their economic structure and provides possibilities for global justice.

In terms of values, the rise of China is morally correct. Historically, the Western powers have enjoyed a more favorable environment, but they developed through ways that many people consider disgraceful. They redirect their conflicts and coordinate their interests to the vast non-Western world. At the same time, they accomplished the primary accumulation of resources through colonialism and wars. Take the United States, for example: it boasts of extraordinary geographical location—with oceans on both its east and its west and no enemy around it. When the European countries were busy fighting against each other and North America's indigenous Indians were no match for the colonists, the United States overtook the leading power status of Europe through a united domestic market and gradual overseas expansion. To the contrary, China, as a newcomer in the modern global system, does not enjoy such a favorable environment. The Westerners have already set the rules and the pattern of interests.

What is more important is that China is facing difficulties other powers never did, both domestically and internationally. It is reasonable for people to worry about China's future based on diverse security threats from the outside world, not to mention the complexity stemming from internal transition, which is discussed later in this chapter. Though the environment is tough, China does not export wars or divert domestic conflicts but solves its problems during industrialization and modernization and within its boundaries while sustaining its high-speed economic development.[2] If China can achieve the modernization of 1.3 billion people on the basis of peace and win-win results, its rise may become much more significant than the rise of any other power in history. That is to say, the rise of China may provide a new mode of development, culture, and value.

However, as one of the power centers in the world, China is facing difficulties concerning development and strategy in response to the vicissitudes of world politics. Therefore, the "China Gospel" theory does not at all mean that China is the messiah. The problems people may encounter need comprehensive consultations and compromises in the context of diverse civilizations. To this end, the Western powers should recognize the momentum of world transformation and give emerging countries some chances to participate in the molding of the system and the right to speak. By way of conclusion, the "China Gospel" theory is a more proper perception of China's international role than either exaggeration or underestimation.

China's Complicated National Condition

The West's failure to understand China has repeatedly undermined its ability to anticipate the direction of China's evolution. Again and again, the West's predictions and beliefs about China have proved incorrect: from political disintegration after the end of the Cold War to the economic collapse later. The West has a long track record of getting China wrong.[3] The failure is due to its frame of reference. The West tends to consider the experiences it obtained under specific conditions as universal truth—and then apply them to other countries, including China, without taking the different conditions of the various countries into consideration. For example, many Westerners believe that China's state power controls everything within the country and that the whole society, a subordinate, is dependent and dull. Some media generalize the words and conduct of some Chinese, based on which they reach an arbitrary conclusion that China is arrogant.

Nevertheless, so complicated is China's society that it reflects practically all the problems and puzzles in the world.[4] In this sense, a clear comprehension of China's complexity is not only crucial to an understanding of China's strategic consideration and policy behaviors but also important to the future of the world. Generally speaking, China gives full scope to its social complexity, thanks to the reform and opening-up policy in more than 30 years. China's modernization contains various stages, processes, multiple forces, and competitive concepts. Due to huge disparities among its different regions, China has to deal with issues of modern, premodern, and postmodern eras. China is also undergoing various interrelated processes such as globalization, industrialization, and democratization at the same time. Different types of forces—including interest groups, netizen politics, bureaucrat politics, and region politics in China—perplex the decision-making process and bring challenges to foreign policy making while inspiring the vigor of the society. A wide range of ideas such as liberalism, new left, and traditionalism also clash on the future path of China.

In addition, the complexity of China's national condition is reflected by the mind-set of ordinary Chinese people. On one hand, the rise of China represents a significant achievement after numerous attempts and failures in more than 100 years. It shows that China, a country with a long history of agricultural tradition, can adapt to industrial civilization. The Chinese people have never been more confident about the great rejuvenation of the nation. On the other hand, industrialization has also given birth to unprecedented problems and challenges. The Chinese people are concerned about the problems brought about by industrialization such as the imbalance of interests, the social conflicts, and the chaotic beliefs, especially when looking at the developed life of the Western world. The complexity of the people's mind-set is also demonstrated by recognition of the outside world. China is eager to win recognition from the outside world through its own efforts, after being at the bottom of the international system for a long time. But China is afraid that it may get trapped in the pitfall of the applause with hidden purposes and undue responsibilities. So exaggerated are reactions that they often get triggered by both criticism *and* appreciation.

Consequently, the complexity of China needs to be analyzed through a dual nature approach. While enjoying high-speed economic development and material wealth accumulation, China is facing unprecedented challenges domestically and internationally. Domestically, the government has to meet people's basic needs and create a harmonious society. On the international level, China has to eliminate other countries' strategic suspicion to sustain a peaceful and stable international environment. So China adopts a twofold foreign policy. With regard to strategies, China adopts a reserved policy, keeping a low profile, biding its time, and focusing on domestic issues. Tactically, China actively tries to achieve some commitment in international issues to preserve its expanded national interests. Overall, China will adhere to an open, cooperative, mutually beneficial view of the overall situation and shoulder due international responsibilities. However, China will take different actions on different issues, especially focusing on the preservation of its core interests and strategic development.

Lack of Institutional Innovations

The mode of economic growth can be divided into three levels according to the driving force—resource input, technological innovation, and institutional innovation. As the supreme way of economic growth, institutional innovation can enhance the efficiency of resource utilization and encourage technological innovations and the application of new technologies. The same goes for competition among nations. In international cooperation, a proper system can provide a widely recognized standard according to which actors can adjust their behaviors toward the outside world. And the effective prediction of gains and loss can reduce the possibilities of betrayal among nations. That is to say, the cost of international cooperation decreases. As for the hegemonic countries, seeking interests through rules and standards is far more effective and stable than through force.

In the economic sphere, the United States blazed its trails through crises and rose to challenges through institutional innovations. The new systems it created gave birth to technologic revolutions and then perpetuated the country's leading status in science and technology. What is more, with the background of modern economy, the system itself becomes productive and generates more interests than technologic advantages. For instance, some systems of no technological significance—such as the chain system of McDonald's, the storage retail system of Walmart, and the assembly lines of Ford—have all brought fundamental changes to the modern economy. In terms of global leadership, the United States has achieved the transition from conquering by force to establishing a so-called fair international system to achieve its special interests. The United States created a distribution regime in global financial and trade areas through the World Bank, the IMF, and the WTO. Within this regime, every country participating in the cooperation will benefit, so these countries are willing to cooperate. As for the United States, it can get the largest share of the benefits. As a matter of fact, the United States, with its own "soft method" of institutional arrangements, managed to open the markets the British Empire had to open by force and were welcomed with cooperation and appreciation, which the British Empire failed to do. All these ease international conflicts and stabilize this entirely new approach toward global hegemony on behalf of the United States.[5]

Resource input has been the main mode of China's economic growth during the past 30 years after the reform and opening up. The intensive resource input and the energy of the system sustain China's rapid and stable economic growth and its important position in global trade, known as the "world's factory." However, there is no denying that this kind of economic development has led to problems such as scarcity of resources, degradation of the natural environment, and damage to the ecosystem, which raise the costs of economic and social development. China is doing well also in technological innovations. As early as the Song Dynasty, there were more than a hundred inventions that were as significant as the Four Great Inventions. They are not as famous as the Four Great Inventions simply because the latter were brought to Europe by the Arabs and known for accelerating modernization there. In the new millennium, China, in pursuit of becoming an innovative country, has embarked on a strategic transformation concerning the mode of economic development and the industrial structure. To this end, China has increased its support of strategic industries and new industries. China now is catching up to or even surpassing the most advanced technologies in the world in such areas as electronic information, aviation and space, and nanotechnology. China's development of high technology has given the country stable midlevel status in global industrial chains.

Nevertheless, China lacks ability in institutional innovations. Domestically, China has to deal with various major issues such as how to achieve sustainable economic development through institutional innovations, how to establish effective channels for expression of interests, and how to handle the relationship between the current system and the emerging social forces. With regard to foreign relations, China mainly focuses on participating in the existing international system. Apparently, China has little power of political rhetoric or capability to act internationally. And innovation of the international system needs further improvement too. Because of inadequate experience and abilities in international affairs, China is incapable of taking advantage of the acknowledged international rules and procedures. So China is not able to actively mold others' expectations. China can only rush around to tackle problems, unable to predict where or when the crisis will break out. The Western world defines the responsibilities and then demands China bear them. This is a reflection of lack of institutional innovations. Therefore, China should learn to promote common ground and institutionalize systems in a Chinese way. For instance, China and the emerging powers can promote gradual reforms of the international order to acquire more quotas of interests and power of rhetoric about, say, international financial reform. At the same time, in response to new issues, China should proactively engage itself in the establishment of a win-win mode of cooperation, such as negotiations on the global climate change.

The Confusion of Multiple Identities

Self-identify is defined as one's self-recognition and orientation, which are important tokens to distinguish one from others. *National identity* has a more multiple nature. It differs in the areas to which the nation pays attention. This multiple nature inevitably causes tensions and conflicts between each identity, and unpredictable troubles and confusions may arise. National identity is relatively stable but also dynamic. It is stable because it is based on a country's history, traditions, and core characteristics. At the same time, identity changes due to environment, development of the society, and frequency of interactions. Actors react to these changes during interactions and then reflect, modify, or change their identities.[6] National identity defines one country's perception of its own interests and policies. Different orientations result in different—even opposite—strategies. Therefore, identity is so important that a false identification might bring about disastrous results for one country such as failure to realize objectives out of overestimation of power or hindrance of national interests in a conservative strategy.

China as a rising power is facing challenges brought by its multiple identities. On one hand, China is in drastic transformation, wherein many forces, issues, and ideas coexist and contest with each other, thus leading to pluralistic self-identification. On the other hand, changes and adjustment are also taking place in the world, with new powers and the old order, and with new issues and old rules in tensions and conflicts, thereby making difficulties for China's identification. So far, there has been four descriptions of China's identity:

1. The largest developing country in the world, while in many aspects it has already become a developed country
2. An important regional power, while it holds wide interests and has huge influence around the world
3. A typical socialist country, while it adopts capitalist characteristics in terms of market system, social values, and consumerism
4. An ancient Confucian civilization, but whose traditions seem to be lost in the market economy and whose modern rules are dominant in society

China thus has dual features in each of those identities, and the features change with interior and exterior factors. This leads to an ambiguity in China's national identity, making it difficult for the outside world to understand China and giving rise to notions like "China Uncertainty Theory" and "China at the Crossroads of the International System." To be specific, such ambiguity in national identity makes the strategy and future of China unpredictable to the outside world. This adds uncertainty to the already complex situation, increasing the doubts of potential rivals and risking the loss of important partners. Also, such ambiguity may leave an impression of opportunism, which will not help China build the image of a responsible power.

In response to the confusion brought by multiple identities, China should first reflect on its traditional diplomatic stances and principles, such as the relation between keeping a low profile and achieving commitments, and the conflicts between noninterference in others' internal affairs and the globalization of national interests. That is to say, China cannot identify itself without eliminating multiple identities. China is a developing power. The fundamental task of China's internal governance and external strategies is to ensure the well-being of 1.3 billion Chinese people. So China's major responsibilities lie within its boundaries. Further, China should seek a stable identity in each field, avoiding free identity transformation, so that China can establish a consistent policy when dealing repeatedly with the same issue, which can enhance trust from the international community. Last, China should attach more internationalism to its national identity. China should provide more international public products—after satisfying its domestic needs—according to its abilities. Also, China should respond to international concerns. Consequently, China can develop the responsible image of a power pursuing win-win results.

Seeking the Future Path

With its growing strength, China has to take on due international responsibilities, which is the expectation from the international community as well as the inevitable choice of China itself toward its own interests. On one hand, the accumulation of China's strength and the expansion of its interests have caused or escalated certain problems in the world, such as the balance between production and consumption and between the supply and demand of global resources. Trivial past issues might attract public attention now simply because China's interests are closely involved. In turn China becomes a center of dispute because of those issues. On the other hand, the current system, under the leadership of the West, is incapable of solving traditional security issues, let alone increasing its response to global challenges. The self-centered mentality and confrontational logic of the Western world are no longer effective when dealing with global issues today. China—with its abundant resources and endowment, national strength, and traditional heritages—can offer enlightening alternatives for reaching the international coexistence of diversified civilizations.

To some extent, it is widely acknowledged that China should assume international responsibilities. However, people argue about which responsibilities to assume, how to fulfill them, and how to balance them between China's own abilities and others' expectations. It is a strategic issue that needs careful examination and comprehensive discussion. If China takes on too many responsibilities, it will exhaust its abilities and may even impede its own development and rise. If China avoids responsibilities, it will not be able to meet external expectations and could be left with a tough international environment. In the long term, this would also hinder China's power of rhetoric and its ability to lead the global agenda.

From a global vision, China should first give priority to its own people. Because a good global image results from effective domestic governance, the greatest responsibility of the Chinese government should be to ensure every Chinese full access to the achievements of modernization and to realize comprehensive development. If China achieved such goals in a peaceful way, it would make more contribution to humankind. Therefore, China's priority is to perfect its institutions and establish a fair and just domestic order under the guidance of a scientific outlook. Only after China has so changed can it influence the world. On the international level, China should differentiate its international responsibilities and different priorities, while resolving contradictory duties and seeking common ones consistent with its interests and power. Furthermore, China should prevent taking on undue responsibilities, typically imposed by Western countries. Most of the time, those responsibilities neither concern China nor are within China's abilities. Last but not least, China should provide more resources and intellectual support for a new mode of global governance.

In order to fulfill its international responsibilities, China should perfect its abilities, hone its mind-set, and develop its institutions. To fulfill international responsibilities, the national strength is the material foundation. China should emphasize coordinated development of soft *and* hard powers, elevating its national strength in an all-round way instead of focusing only on economic development. That way the international community will be able to examine China's power from an objective point of view instead of through its imagination. As for mind-set, China should not avoid international responsibilities under the pretext of "Conspiracy Theory," because that would reflect a weak mind-set and a lack of confidence. The proper attitude should be to keep calm and take on due responsibilities while feeling confident but not being imprudent. In institutional respect, China should optimize cooperation among different social groups and government departments. China should also propose a continuous stance in foreign policy. All in all, a rising China has become a constructive power in promoting global peace and development. It will shoulder due responsibilities concerning security, economy, and development. And although the road ahead may be long and winding, China will march along with firm and powerful steps as a responsible power.

NOTES

Chapter 1

1. Henry A. Kissinger, *Diplomacy*, New York: Simon & Schuster, 1994, p. 17.
2. See Robert Gilpin, *War and Change in World Politics*, New York: Cambridge University Press, 1995, Chapter V.
3. Wang Xiaozong, Which Province's GDP Is Most Valuable? *China Economic Weekly*, 2011, Issue 8, p. 32.
4. See Liu Liandi, *Selected Important Documents on China-US Relations*, Beijing: Current Affairs Press, 1996, pp. 391–392.
5. Ibid., p. 451.
6. See Martin Jacques, *When China Rules the World: The Rise of the Middle Kingdom and the End of the Western World*. Allen Lane, 2009.
7. Rana Foroohar, "It's China's World. We're Just Living in It," http://www.newsweek.com/2010/03/11/it-s-china-s-world-we-re-just-living-in-it.html.
8. Xin Zhiming, "Yuan and Absurdity of U.S. Demand," *China Daily*, July 29, 2010, p. 9.

Chapter 2

1. Lao Tsu, *The Tao Te Ching*, Chapter 25, Zhonghua Book Company, December 2008, p. 64.
2. *Analects of Confucius*, trans. Zhang Yanying, Beijing: Zhonghua Book Company, 2006, p. 199.
3. Ibid., p. 250.
4. Ibid., p. 241.
5. Ibid., p. 44.
6. Ibid., p. 47.
7. Ibid., p. 275.
8. Ibid., p. 83.
9. See "A Changing China in a Changing World—Address by Yang Jiechi, Minister of Foreign Affairs of the People's Republic of China, at the Munich Security Conference," http://www.china-embassy.org/chn/zt/231432/xw1/t657032.htm.

10. *Analects of Confucius*, p. 195.

11. Ibid., p. 58.

12. See Chen Xiangyang, "Practical Benevolent Rule and Good Neighbor Diplomacy," *Journal of Jiangnan Social University*, 2006(6).

13. Guidance of the Report to the 17th CPC, Beijing: Learning Press and Party Reading-Material Press, 2007, p. 44.

14. See Yang Jiechi, "Interviews with Ministers of the Republic," *Legal Daily*, August 25, 2009.

15. See Hu Jintao, "Cooperation Generates a Better Future—The Speech at the 64th UN General Assembly Debate," Xinhua net, September 24, 2009.

16. See Zhang Xiaotong, "China's Propositions in Hu's Time," *Outlook Weekly*, 2009(47).

17. Ibid.

18. See Hu Jintao, "Join Hands to Address Climate Challenges—The Speech at the Opening Plenary Session of the United Nations Summit on Climate Change," Xinhua net, September 23, 2009.

19. "Hu Jintao, Speech to the Conference to Mark the 30th Anniversary of the Convening of the 3rd Plenary Session of the 11th Communist Party of China (CPC) Central Committee," Xinhua net, December 18, 2009.

20. See Guidance of the Report to the 17th CPC, p. 43.

21. See "WB Says China's Poverty Line Is Too Low Compared to International Standards," *China Youth News*, April 9, 2009.

22. According to the CNR News of VOC in February 3, 2010, NEB's data showed that China's foreign dependency rate of oil had reached 51.3 percent, breaking the public psychological barrier of 50 percent for the first time.

Chapter 3

1. See Zheng Yongnian, "China: The Mind-set and Responsibilities of a Great Power," Tong Zhou Gong Jin, 2008(8).

2. See Rep. Henry Hyde, "China's Responsibility in a Multipolar World," *Asian Wall Street Journal*, December 3, 2004.

3. Ibid.

4. See Anver Versi, "China Is Good for Africa," *African Business*, March 2007, p. 11.

5. See Wang Xinjun, "Military Transparency—China's Solemn Commitment," *People's Daily Overseas Edition*, September 7, 2007.

6. See Bates Gill, Dan Blumenthal, Michael Swaine, and Jessica Tuchman Mathews: China as a Responsible Stakeholder, Monday, June 11,

2007, Washington, D.C., http://www.carnegieendowment.org/
events/?fa=eventDetail&id=998.

7. See Zhao Xiaozhuo, "Bates Gill: We Are Increasing Studies on China,"
April 10, 2009.

8. See "The World Famous Chinese Blue Helmets during 20 Years in UN
Peacekeeping Operations," *PLA Daily*, April 26, 2010.

9. See Tian Jin, and Yu Mengjia, *China in the UN: Work Together for a Better
World*, Beijing: World Affairs Press, 1999, p. 40.

10. See Elizabeth Economy, and Michel Oksenberg, eds., *China Joins the
World*, Beijing: Xiahua Press, 2001, p. 57.

11. See Zhao Lei, *Constructing Peace: China's Diplomacy in the UN*, Beijing:
Jiuzhou Press, 2007, pp. 199–201.

12. See "The Images of China's Peacekeeping Staff in the Last 20 Years,"
People's Daily, April 2, 2010.

12b. "China's 'blue helmets' forces pours the beautiful flowers of peace with
blood," *People's Daily* overseas edition, July 31, 2007.

13. United Nations Peacekeeping Operations: Principles and Guideline,
United Nations, Department of Peacekeeping Operations Department
of Field Support, January 2010, p. 31, http://www.un.org/zh/documents/
view_doc.asp?url=//pbpu.unlb.org/pbps/Library/Capstone_Doctrine_ENG
.pdf.

14. See Ma Xiaochun, and Wu Xu, "Retrospection on the UN Peacekeeping
Operations," http://www.chinamil.com.cn/item/peace/txt/19.htm.

15. See Wang Liang, "China Trains Its Troops with Peacekeeping Missions,"
Dongfang Daily, June 19, 2007.

16. See Note 8.

17. See Zheng Nan, "China Is Crucial in the UN Peacekeeping Operations,"
July 30, 2010, http://www.unmultimedia.org/radio/chinese/detail/139918
.html.

18. See "The UN Secretary General Expects Better Partnership with China,"
Xinhua net, June 28, 2008.

19. See Li Hong, "The Progress of International Nuclear Armament:
Opportunities and Challenges," *Foreign Affairs Journal* (Chinese People's
Institute of Foreign Affairs), 2009(95).

20. See Hu Jintao, "Forging a World of Common Security Together—The
Speech on the UN Nuclear Non-proliferation and Disarmament Summit,"
People.com.cn, September 25, 2009.

21. See Liu Zhenmin, "Nuclear Energy to Promote the Well-being of Human
Beings by Actively Stimulating International Nuclear Disarmament and
Non-proliferation," *Qiushi*, 2010(11).

22. See State Council Information Office, "White Paper on China's Non-proliferation Policy," December 3, 2003.

23. See "Regulations on Nuclear Export Control of the People's Republic of China, http://www.miit.gov.cn/n11293472/n11294912/n11296257/11936718.html.

24. See "China's Contributions to Nuclear Disarmament and Nuclear Non-proliferation," http://www.china.com.cn/chinese/zhuanti/hcj/860967.htm.

25. See "The DPRK Nuclear Issue," http://news.xinhuanet.com/ziliao.

26. See "The DPRK Nuclear Issue," http://news.xinhuanet.com/ziliao/2003-01/08/content_683434.htm.

27. See "Wu Dawei on the Three Tasks of the Six-Party Talks," http://news.xinhuanet.com/world/2007-03/09/content_5824396.htm.

28. See Note 25.

29. See "International Reviews: the DPRK Nuclear Issue—the Priority of Rice's Visit in Asia Xinhuanet, July 13, 2005.

30. See Fu Ying, "Friendship and Partnership with Neighboring Countries—China's Neighboring Relations," *Current Affairs*, Publicity Department of the Central Committee of the CPC, December 18, 2003.

31. See Zhu Weilie, "The Mechanism and Experience of China's Hotspot Diplomacy," *International Observation*, 2009(1).

32. See "Foreign Ministry Spokesman Qin Gang's Remark on the Latest UN Resolution to the Iran Nuclear Issue on Press Conference," http://www.fmprc.gov.cn/chn/pds/wjdt/fyrbt/.

33. See "The Foreign Ministry Chief Executive of Political Affairs Conference among Six Countries Convened in Shanghai," Xinhua net, April 16, 2008.

34. See "Six Countries Drafting a Sanction against Iran Does Not Mean the End of a Diplomatic Solution to the Issue," Xinhua net, May 19, 2010.

35. See "China Stated That the Discussion in the UN Security Council Does Not Put an End to the Diplomatic Efforts to the Iran Nuclear Issue," Xinhua net, May 19, 2010.

36. See Information Office of the State Council, " 'East Turkistan' Forces have to Bear the Consequences," *People's Daily*, January 22, 2002.

37. Tibetan Youth Congress (TYC), established in 1970, is a terrorist group of national separatism, advocating "the complete independence of Tibet." TYC launched the notorious "3·14" incident. According to statistics, TYC destroyed and burned 56 vehicles, burned or stabbed 13 innocent civilians to death, injured tens of policemen. And it committed over 300 crimes of arson and burned down 214 residences and shops. It is of high danger to society.

38. See Wang Yi, "New Challenge, New Concepts—Global Anti-terrorism and China's Policies," http://www.fmprc.gov.cn.

39. See "The UN against Terrorism," http://www.un.org/chinese/terrorism/.

40. See "China Is against Double Standards on Anti-terrorism," http://news .xinhuanet.com/misc/2005-09/05/content_3447367.htm.

41. See "Hu Jintao: Eradicate the Root Cause of Terrorism," http://www .chinanews.com.cn/n/2003-10-21/26/359607.html.

42. See "The Ministry of Public Security Believes Terrorism Has Acquired New Characteristics and Threatened China," cps.com.cn, August 30, 2005.

43. See Yang Jiechi, "China's Diplomacy Since the Reform and Opening-up," *Seeking Truth*, 2008(8).

44. Hu Jintao, "Promote Peace in Middle East and Harmony in the World," *People's Daily*, April 23, 2006.

45. See China-Arab Cooperation Forum Official Website, http://www.cascf .org/chn/gylt/#b.

46. Five Proposals: First, respecting the history, taking each other's concern into account, and following the direction of peaceful negotiations. Second, giving up violence, removing interference, and believing in peaceful negotiations. Third, pushing forward the peace process in an all-around and balanced manner and creating a favorable atmosphere for peace talks. Fourth, promoting development, strengthening cooperation, and consolidating the foundation of peace talks. Fifth, reaching consensus, increasing input, and strengthening guarantee for the peace talks. See "Yang Jiechi on China's Position on the Middle East Issue," http://news.xinhua net.com/newscenter/2007-11/28/ content_7157134.htm.

47. See "Respecting the Diversity of Culture—Prime Minister Wen Jiabao's Speech at the Headquarters of the League of Arab States in Cairo," Xinhua net, November 7, 2009.

48. See "The UN Senior Official Spoke Highly of China's Role in the Darfur Issue," Xinhua net, September 11, 2007.

49. See "President Hu Jintao Met with Sudan President Bashir," Xinhua net, February 2, 2007.

50. See "Foreign Ministry Spokeswoman Jiang Yu on Regular Press Conference on May 10, 2007," http://www.fmprc.gov.cn/chn/pds/wjdt/fyrbt/t317761. htm.

51. See the Sudan Darfur Page of the UN Website, http://www.un.org/chinese/ ha/issue/sudan/un.shtm.

52. See "The US Ambassador Supports China's Role in the Darfur Region," *China Daily*, April 12, 2007.

Chapter 4

1. Many scholars have debated whether China can save the world. For example, see Bill Powell, "Can China Save the World?" *Time*, http://www.time.com/time/magazine/article/0,9171,1913638-1,00.html, August 10, 2009; Michael Wesley, "Made in China," *Griffith Review*, http://www.griffithreview.com/edition-25-after-the-crisis/227-essay/688-wesley25.html.

2. For study of the China Threat theory, see Chen Jibing, *Next Stop: China*, Shanghai: Wenhui, 2008, pp. 129–175; Lu Gang and Guo Xuetang, *Interpreting "China Threat,"* Beijing: Academia Press, 2004; Shi Aiguo, *Pride and Prejudice—Orientalism and the China Threat Theory in the United States*, Guangzhou: Sun Yat-sen University Press, 2004.

3. See Minxin Pei, "China: The Big Free Rider," *Newsweek*, http://www.newsweek.com/2010/01/21/china-the-big-free-rider.html, January 22, 2010.

4. As director of the United States Peter G. Peterson Institute for International Economics, Fred Bergsten issued "A Partnership of Equals: How Washington Should Respond to China's Economic Challenge" in *Foreign Affairs* in the summer of 2008, putting forward the idea of G-2 for the first time. He believed that China and the United States should not dwell on or complain about each other on the many issues in bilateral relations but should develop a true partnership to achieve joint leadership of the global economic system. See Fred Bergsten, "A Partnership of Equals: How Washington Should Respond to China's Economic Challenge," *Foreign Affairs*, Vol. 87, July/August 2008.

5. Niall Ferguson, "Buy Chimerican," *Los Angeles Times*, http://www.latimes.com/news/printedition/asection/la-oe-ferguson5mar05,0,3424390.column, March 5, 2007.

6. See Jin Canrong and Liu Shiqiang, "China-US Relations Since Obama Came into Power," *American Studies Quarterly*, 2009(4).

7. See Robert B. Zoellick and Justin Yifu Lin, "Recovery Rides on the 'G2,'" *Washington Post*, http://www.washingtonpost.com/wp-dyn/content/article/2009/03/05/AR2009030502887.html, March 6, 2009.

8. See Elizabeth C. Economy and Adam Segal, "The G2 Mirage: Why the United States and China Are Not Ready to Upgrade Ties," *Foreign Affairs*, Vol. 88, May/June 2009.

9. See Morton Abramowitz, "Triple Threat," *National Interests*, http://nationalinterest.org/article/triple-threat-3110, May 1, 2009.

10. See Cai Weiwei, "Why China Does Not Recognize G2," http://www.cass.net.cn/file/20090602234664.html, June 2, 2009.

10b. China's Poverty Alleviation and Development Report: China's Successful Poverty Alleviation Accelerated the World's Poverty Alleviation Process, http://news.xinhuanet.com/newscenter/2007-10/17/content_6896208.htm.

11. "The United Nations Millennium Development Goals Report 2010," Foreword, p. 3, http://www.un.org/chinese/millenniumgoals/pdf/MDG-Report2010Zh-lowers.pdf.

12. See Food and Agriculture Organization of the United Nations, "The State of Food Insecurity in the World: Economic Crises—Impacts and Lessons Learned," ftp://ftp.fao.org/docrep/fao/012/i0876c/i0876c.pdf, pp. 8–11.

13. See Fan Xiaojian, "Sixty Years: Key Actions of Poverty Alleviation and Development," *Seeking Truth*, 2009(20).

14. See "United Nations Officials Say That China Plays an Important Role in the World Poverty Reduction," Xinhua net, February 17, 2010.

15. See "Steady Development of China-Africa Economic and Trade Cooperation," Website of Ministry of Commerce, November 4, 2009.

16. For a discussion of neocolonialism in the West, see Zhang Shunhong, Meng Qinglong, and Bi Jiankang, *Neo-Colonialism of Britain and the United States*, Beijing: Social Science Academic Press, 2007.

17. See Tunde Adelakun, "Is the Influence of China Growing in Nigeria?" http://www.helium.com/items/439062, August 23, 2009.

18. The eight measures are as follows: (1) Expand the scale of aid to Africa. Double China's scale of assistance to African countries in 2006 by 2009. (2) Provide 3 billion U.S. dollars of preferential loans and 2 billion U.S. dollars of preferential export buyer's credit to African countries in the next three years. (3) Establish a China-Africa development fund that will reach 5 billion U.S. dollars to encourage Chinese enterprises to invest in Africa and provide support to them. (4) Build a conference center for the African Union to support African countries in their efforts to strengthen themselves through unity and support the process of African integration. (5) Cancel debt in the form of all the interest-free government loans that matured at the end of 2005 owed by the heavily indebted poor countries and the least-developed counties in Africa that have diplomatic relations with China. (6)

Further open up China's market to Africa by increasing from 190 to over 440 the number of export items to China receiving zero-tariff treatment from the least-developed countries in Africa having diplomatic ties with China. (7) Establish three to five economic and trade cooperation zones in Africa in the next three years. (8) Over the next three years, train 15,000 African professionals; send 100 senior agricultural experts to Africa; set up 10 special agricultural technology demonstration centers in Africa; build 30 hospitals in Africa and provide 300 million RMB of grant for providing artemisinin and building 30 malaria prevention and treatment centers to fight malaria in Africa; dispatch 300 youth volunteers to Africa; build 100 rural schools in Africa; and increase the number of Chinese government scholarships to African students from the current 2,000 per year to 4,000 per year by 2009.

19. The eight new measures taken by the Chinese government to promote China-Africa cooperation are as follows: (1) Propose to establish a China-Africa partnership in responding to climate change, to hold nonscheduled senior officials' consultations, and to strengthen cooperation in satellite weather monitoring, development and utilization of new energy, prevention and control of desertification and urban environmental protection, etc. Build 100 clean energy projects for Africa covering solar power, biogas, and small hydropower. (2) Enhance cooperation with Africa in science and technology. Propose to launch a China-Africa science and technology partnership, under which we will carry out 100 joint demonstration projects on scientific and technological research, receive 100 African postdoctoral fellows to conduct scientific research in China, and assist them in going back and serving their home countries. (3) Help Africa build up financing capacity. Provide 10 billion U.S. dollars in concessional loans to African countries and support Chinese financial institutions in setting up a 1-billion-U.S.-dollar special loan for small and medium-size African businesses. For the heavily indebted poor countries and the least-developed countries in Africa having diplomatic relations with China, cancel their debts associated with interest-free government loans due to mature by the end of 2009. (4) Further open up China's market to African products. Phase in zero-tariff treatment for 95 percent of the products from the least-developed African counties having diplomatic relations with China, starting with 60 percent of the products by 2010. (5) Further enhance cooperation with Africa in agriculture. Increase the number of agricultural technology demonstration centers built by China in Africa to 20, send 50 agricultural technology teams to Africa, and train 2,000 agricultural technology personnel for Africa in order to help strengthen Africa's ability to ensure food security. (6) Deepen cooperation in medical

care and health. Provide medical equipment and antimalaria materials worth 500 million RMB to the 30 hospitals and 30 malaria prevention and treatment centers built by China and train 3,000 doctors and nurses for Africa. (7) Enhance cooperation in human resources development and education. Build 50 China-Africa friendship schools and train 1,500 school principals and teachers for African countries. By 2012, increase the number of Chinese government scholarships to Africa to 5,500. Train a total of 20,000 professionals in various fields for Africa over the next three years. (8) Expand people-to-people and cultural exchanges. Propose to launch a China-Africa joint research and exchange program that will enable scholars and research organizations to have more exchanges and cooperation, share development experience, and provide intellectual support for formulating better cooperation policies by the two sides.

20. See "Expand the Scale of Assistance to Africa and Comprehensively Improve China-Africa Economic and Trade Cooperation," http://www.gov.cn/gzdt/2010-01/06/content_1504272.htm, January 6, 2010.

21. Ibid.

22. Cited in Chen Jibing, *Next Stop: China*, p. 163.

23. The eight principles of foreign aid announced by the People's Republic of China are as follows: (1) The Chinese government never regards aid to other countries as a kind of unilateral alms but as something mutual based on the principle of equality and mutual benefit. (2) The Chinese government respects the sovereignty of the recipient countries when extending foreign assistance and never attaches any conditions or asks for any privileges. (3) The Chinese government provides financial assistance in the form of interest-free loans or low-interest loans and extends the repayment period if necessary to minimize the burden on the recipient countries. (4) The foreign aid from the Chinese government is not intended to make the recipient countries dependent on China but to help them embark on taking the self-reliant and independent path of development. (5) The Chinese government tries to help the recipient countries build projects that are low in investment and quick in effect so that the countries can increase revenue and accumulate capital. (6) The Chinese government provides the best-quality equipment and materials it can produce on its own and in accordance with international market prices. Replacement is guaranteed if the equipment and materials provided by the Chinese government do not meet the agreed specifications and quality. (7) The Chinese government ensures that personnel in the recipient countries grasp the technology when providing any kind of technical assistance. (8) Chinese experts sent to the recipient countries enjoy the same treatment as those of the recipient countries and no special requirements are allowed.

24. See Zhang Qingmin, "From 'Internationalism' to 'Equality and Mutual Benefit': Evolution of China's Foreign Aid Policies," http://www.china.com.cn/news/60years/2009-08/28/content_18422630.htm, August 28, 2009.

25. Ibid.

26. Zhou Qi, "China's Foreign Aid and Human Rights Concerns—Thoughts Provoked by Darfur Humanitarian Crisis," http://www.humanrights-china.org/cn/xsdt/xscg/t20080611_364239.htm, June 11, 2008.

26b. White Paper on China's Foreign Aid, http://www.chinanews.com/gn/2011/04-21/2989430_3.shtml.

27. See "Achievements Received in Eight Fields during the Sixty Years of China's Foreign Aid," http://www.chinanews.com.cn/cj/2010/08-13/2466843.shtml, August 13, 2010.

28. Information Office of the State Council of the People's Republic of China: "China's Human Rights Situation," http://news.xinhuanet.com/ziliao/2003-01/20/content_697545.htm.

29. See Wang Chen, "China's Human Rights Have Achieved Historical Development in Sixty Years," *Seeking Truth*, 2009(21).

30. Information Office of the State Council of the People's Republic of China: National Human Rights Action Plan of China (2009–2010), http://www.humanrights.cn/cn/rqsy/tj/1/t20090413_438878.htm.

31. Ibid., p. 13.

32. Ibid.

33. See Yan Yuanping, "Those Days in Benin—Profile of Ningxia Medical Assistance to Benin for Thirty Years," *Communist*, 2008(4).

34. See "Ningxia Medical Aid Team to Benin: Going to Benin with Universal Fraternity," http://www.nxnet.net/zhuanti/2008zt/gaige30/gaige18/200812/t20081216_394161.htm, December 16, 2008.

35. Ibid.

36. See Lü Shuqun and Wu Qiong, eds., *Going to Benin*, Yinchuan: Ningxia People's Publishing House, 2003, p. 29.

37. See "Gao Qiang's Speech at the 45th Anniversary Commemoration and Commendatory Conference of National Foreign Medical Aids Teams," http://www.moh.gov.cn/publicfiles/business/htmlfiles/mohzcfgs/s6774/200901/38875.htm.

38. See the Ministry of Health of the People's Republic of China: "The Thirty Years of Reform and Opening-Up of Health of China: Exchanges and Cooperation in Health," http://www.moh.gov.cn/publicfiles/business/htmlfiles/mohbgt/s9453/200901/38681.htm.

39. See "China's Medical Aid Team in Niger Offers Medical Services for Local Residents," http://www.acucn.com/sub/zhongfei/zhenjiu/200611/1961.html.

40. The Health Department of Jiangsu Province, ed., *Glorious History—Collected Works for the Fortieth Anniversary of Foreign Aid Teams of Jiangsu Province*, Nanjing: Jiangsu Science and Technology Publishing House, 2004. Cited in Li Anshan, "The History, Scale and Influence of Chinese Medical Aid Teams Abroad," *Foreign Affairs Review*, 2009(1).

Chapter 5

1. President Hu's speech at the conference on the 30th anniversary of reform and opening-up," *China Daily*, December 18, 2008.
2. *BRICs* refers to Brazil, Russia, India, and China. "Next-11" refers to Pakistan, Egypt, Indonesia, Iran, the Republic of Korea, the Philippines, Mexico, Bangladesh, Nigeria, Turkey, and Vietnam. "VISTA" refers to Vietnam, Indonesia, South Africa, Turkey, and Argentina.
3. According to updated IMF statistics, the proportion of U.S. dollars in the international reserve currencies is 63 percent.
4. In IMF, the United States holds 16.77 percent of the voting rights, and the proportions of those of Japan, Germany, France, and Britain are 6.02 percent, 5.88 percent, 4.85 percent, and 4.85 percent, respectively. The five developed countries control 38.37 percent of the voting rights. In the World Bank, the United States holds 16.36 percent of the voting rights, and the proportions of those of Japan, Germany, France, and Britain are 7.85 percent, 4.48 percent, 4.30 percent, and 4.30 percent, respectively. The five countries control 37.29 percent of the voting rights.
5. See Zhu Guangyao, "Promote the Reform of the International Financial System and Establish a New International Financial Order," *China Finance*, 2010(3).
6. The speech President Hu Jintao delivered at the G-20 Financial Summit on November 15, 2008.
7. Since RMB exchange rate reform in July 2005, the RMB exchange rate appreciated by more than 21 percent, but instead, China's international payments surplus expanded from 223.8 billion U.S. dollars in 2005 to 445.3 billion U.S. dollars in 2007, 445.1 billion U.S. dollars in 2008, and 393.2 billion U.S. dollars in 2009.
8. *G-8* refers to the United States, Britain, France, Germany, Italy, Canada, Japan, and Russia.
9. *G-20* consists of G-8 and 11 important emerging industrial countries (China, Argentina, Australia, Brazil, India, Indonesia, Mexico, the Republic of Korea, Saudi Arabia, South Africa, and Turkey) and the EU.

10. See "Take Efforts to Promote Growth and Balanced Development," delivered by President Hu on the third G-20 Financial Summit, September 25, 2009.
11. See the speech delivered by President Hu on the fourth G-20 Financial Summit in Toronto, June 27, 2010.
12. "The Press Conference by MOC on the commercial work of the first half year and answering reporters' questions," www.gov.cn, July 20, 2010.
13. See Huang Zhixiong, "The Analysis of Doha Round Negotiations of WTO and China's Multilateral Diplomacy." *International Forum*, 2008(6).
14. Research Group of China's Economic Growth and Macroeconomic Stability, "Global Imbalances, Financial Crisis and China's Economic Recovery," *Economic Studies*, 2009(5).
15. The adjustment and promotion plan for 10 industries, passed in 2009, involves the automobile industry, steel industry, textile industry, equipment manufacturing industry, shipbuilding industry, electronic information industry, light industry, petrochemical industry, ferrous metals industry, and logistics industry.
16. Premier Wen Jiaobao received the special interview from Xinhua Agency on December 27, 2009.
17. See Ma kai, "On Advancing the Adjustment of Economic Structure Facing the Global Financial Crisis," *Decision Guide*, 2010(1).
18. Hao Yanfei, "Opportunities and Challenges of China's New Energy Development," *China Technology Investment*, 2010(7).
19. Zheng Xianwu, "Inter-regional Cooperation and East Asian Regionalism," *International View*, 2009(6).
20. See the speech delivered by Yang Jiechi on the China-ASEAN Foreign Ministers Meeting in Hanoi of Vietnam on July 22, 2010.
21. See Wang Li, "Xi Jinping Accepted a Joint Interview from in-Beijing Media of Japan and the Republic of Korea," *People's Daily*, December 13, 2009.

Chapter 6

1. See Mancur Olson, *The Logic of Collective Action: Public Goods and the Theory of Groups*, trans. Chen Yu, Guo Yufeng, and Li Chongxin, Shanghai: Sdxjoint Publishing Company, 1995, p. 14.
2. See Hu Angang, *Roadmap of China's Rising*, Beijing: Beijing University Press, 2007, p. 27.
3. See Hedley Bull, *The Anarchical Society: A Study of Order in World Politics*, trans. Zhang Xiaoming, Beijing: World Affairs Press, 2003, p. 13.
4. See Aristotle, *Politics*, trans. Wu Shoupeng, Beijing: Commercial Press, 1965, p. 7.

5. Li Tiecheng, ed., *Getting Closer to the United Nations*, Beijing: People's Press, 2008, p. 367.

6. See "Position Paper of the People's Republic of China on the United Nations Reforms," http://www.fmprc.gov.cn/chn/pds/ziliao/zt/ ywzt/2005year/zgylhg/t199083.htm, June 7, 2005.

7. See Hu Jintao, "Making Efforts to Build a Harmonious World of Enduring Peace and Common Prosperity," http://news.xinhuanet.com/world/2005 -09/16/content_3496858.htm, September 16, 2005.

8. The six initiatives for achieving the Millennium Development Goals are as follows: (1) Double the number of agricultural technology demonstration centers, agricultural experts, and technical staff in the recipient countries in the next five years and provide agricultural training in China to 3,000 people in developing countries. (2) Donate 30 million U.S. dollars to FAO to establish a trust fund to help developing countries enhance agricultural productivity. (3) Provide exports and assistance to countries facing food shortages. (4) Provide 10,000 scholarships to students in developing countries to study in China in the next five years. (5) Exempt debt—in the form of the interest-free loans—that matures at the end of this year owed by the least-developed countries and conduct zero-tariff treatment to 95 percent of the products from the least-developed countries. (6) Help build a hundred small hydropower, solar, methane, and other small-scale clean energy projects in developing countries in the next five years.

9. See Men Honghua, "China's International Strategic Adjustment and UN Diplomacy (1949–2009)," UN Association of China, ed., *China's UN Diplomacy*, Beijing: World Affairs Press, 2009, p. 42.

10. See Yang Zewei, ed., *International Law Studies on United Nations Reforms*, Wuhan: Wuhan University Press, 2009, pp. 337–338.

11. See Xin Benjian, "Emissions Reductions in China and Echo from the International Community." *People's Daily* Overseas Edition, August 6, 2010.

12. See Liu Changyong, "Xiaotangshan 'SARs' Hospital Built in Seven Days and Nights," *China Economic Weekly*, 2009 (39).

13. See Li Wenzhao, "How Far Has China Gone from SARS to Influenza H1N1?" *Beijing News*, May 16, 2009.

14. See Chen Zhu, "Speech at the Mobilization Teleconference of Vaccine Immunization of Influenza H1N1," http://www.moh.gov.cn/publicfiles/ business/htmlfiles/chenz/pldjh/200911/44296.htm, November 3, 2009.

15. See http://www.fmprc.gov.cn/chn/pds/ziliao/tytj/.

16. See "The Issues of Biological and Chemical Weapons," White Paper on China's Endeavors for Arms Control, Disarmament and Non-proliferation, http://news.xinhuanet.com/mil/2005-09/01/content_3429141_2.htm, September 1, 2005.

17. See Ambassador Cheng Jingye, head of the Chinese delegation, speech at the Ninth Annual Conference of the revised Landmine Protocol in Geneva, Switzerland in 2007, http://www.chinanews.com.cn/gn/news/2007/11 -14/1077059.shtml, November 14, 2007.

18. See Song Hong, "China and the WTO: A Process of Mutual Learning, Adaptation and Promotion," Wang Yizhou, ed., *Construction in Contradiction: a Multiple Insight into Relationship between China and Key International Organizations*, Beijing: China Development Press, 2003, pp. 217–219.

19. See White Paper on China's Intellectual Property Rights Protection in 2009, http://www.nipso.cn/onews.asp?id=9482.

20. "The upgrade of the State Environmental Protection Administration to the Ministry of Environmental Protection was described as the 'highlight of the highlights' of the year's ministerial reform by the French European Times," http://www.china.com.cn/tech/zhuanti/wyh/2008 -03/15/ content_12702315.htm, March 15, 2008.

21. See Robert O. Keohane and Joseph S. Nye, *Power and Interdependence*, 3rd ed., trans. Men Honghua, Beijing: Beijing University Press, 2002, pp. 25–26.

22. See Robert O.Keohane, *After Hegemony: Cooperation and Discord in the World Political Economy*, trans. Su Changhe, Xin Qiang, and He Yao, Shanghai: Shanghai People's Publishing House, 2006, p. 61.

23. See Pang Geping, "China-ASEAN Free Trade Area Creates New Business Opportunities," *People's Daily*, July 26, 2010.

24. The strict rules are as follows: Obsolete and banned constructions and those that do not conform to the industrial policies shall not be approved; projects that cause environmental pollution, with low quality as well as high energy and material consumption, in particular those that do not meet the standards of pollutant emission, shall not be approved; projects whose environmental quality does not meet the requirements of the environmental function and those that exceed the quota limit shall not be approved; projects located in nature reserves, core zones, and buffer zones shall not be approved. Projects related to drinking water source reserves, nature reserves, scenic areas, and important ecological function areas shall be strictly limited; industries with high energy consumption shall be strictly controlled, and projects that have been eliminated shall be prevented from being reapproved on grounds of technological innovation or stimulating domestic demand; and total pollutant emissions will be taken as constraints for the development of regions, industries, and businesses in strict accordance with overall control.

25. "Hu Jintao, Wu Bangguo, Wen Jiabao, Jia Qinglin, Xi Jinping, Li Keqiang, He Guoqiang, and Zhou Yongkang Visit the 2009 China International Energy-Saving and New Energy Technologies Expo," *People's Daily*, March 21, 2009.

26. See the answer by Zhang Ping, director of National Development and Reform Commission of the People's Republic of China, at the press conference about China's macroeconomic policy at the third session of the 11th National People's Congress, http://2010lianghui.people.com.cn /GB/181620/181621/183395/183397/index.html, March 6, 2010.

27. "The Notice by the National Development and Reform Commission on Approving Wuhan City Circle and Changsha, Zhuzhou, and Xiangtan Urban Agglomeration to Be the Country's Energy-Saving and Environmentally Friendly Pilot Area of Comprehensive Coordinated Reform on Social Construction," http://wh2xsh.wh.gov.cn/gjw j/2008/08/04110953.html, December 23, 2008.

28. See Department of Rural and Social Development, Ministry of Science and Technology, and the Administrative Center for China's Agenda 21(ACCA21), China National Sustainable Pilot Areas Review Report (1986–2006), Beijing: Social Sciences Academic Press, 2007, pp. 15–18.

29. See the Editorial Board's Annual Policy Report of the China Council for International Cooperation on Environment and Development, ed., Strategic Transformation of China's Environment and Development Mode, Beijing: China Environmental Science Press, 2007, p. 19.

30. See Sun Liping, "China's Considering Evaluation of Local Officials with 'Green Development Indicators' in the 12th Five-Year Plan," http://politics. people.com.cn/GB/1026/12049403.html, July 4, 2010.

31. See "The United Nations Environment Programme: Germany, China, and the Republic of Korea Are the Most Outstanding Examples in Enhancing Climate Accountability Since Copenhagen," http://www.un.org/zh/ climatechange/newsdetails.asp?newsID=13341, April 21, 2010.

32. See Wen Jiabao, "Reaching Consensus and Strengthening Cooperation to Promote the Historical Process of Responding to Climate Change," *People's Daily*, December 19, 2009.

33. See Copenhagen Accord, Article V.

34. For a sophisticated study of the fairness and justice of per-capita emissions standards, see the series of articles by Pan Jiahua: Pan Jiahua, "A Conceptual Framework for Understanding Human Development Potential with Empirical Analysis of Global Demand for Carbon Emissions," *Social Sciences in China*, 2002(6); Pan Jiahua, "The Carbon Budget for Basic Needs Satisfaction and Implications for International Equity and

Sustainability," *World Economics and Politics*, 2008(1); Pan Jiahua and Chen Ying, "The Carbon Budget Scheme: An Institutional Framework for a Fair and Sustainable World Climate Regime," *Social Sciences in China*, 2009(5); Pan Jiahua and Zheng Yan, "Responsibility and Individual Equity for Carbon Emissions Rights," *World Economics and Politics*, 2009(10); Pan Jiahua, "Carbon Emissions and Development Rights," Yang Jiemian, ed., *Global Climate Change Diplomacy and China's Policy*, Beijing: Current Affairs Publishing House, 2009, pp. 241–256.

35. See Zou Ji, "Innovation in International Mechanisms for Technology Development and Transfer in Climate Change," *Environmental Protection*, 2008(5).

36. See Anthony Giddens, *The Politics of Climate Change*, Cambridge, U.K.: Polity Press, 2009, p. 220.

37. See Xu Qinhua and Wang Hongjun, "APEC Multilateral Energy Cooperation and China," *Contemporary International Relations*, 2009(12).

38. "The Network of Asia-Pacific Forest Rehabilitation and Sustainable Management Launched Today," http://politics.people.com.cn/GB/1026 /8105005.html, September 25, 2008.

Chapter 7

1. See Jin Canrong, and Liu Shiqiang, "Farewell Western Centralism—Reflections on the Current International System and the Future," *International Review*, 2010 (2).

2. See Zhang Weiwei, "China's Pattern in Response to the Global Challenges," *Contemporary Chinese History Studies*, 2008(2).

3. See Martin Jacques, "Understanding China," *Los Angeles Times*, http:// articles.latimes.com/2009/nov/22/opinion/la-oe-jacques22-2009nov22.

4. Analysis of the multidimensional identities and the various processes of China. See Yuan Peng, "The Vicissitudes of the International System and China's Strategies," *Contemporary International Relations*, 2009(11).

5. See Jin Canrong, "Why Is the U.S. Welcomed?" *Renmin Luntan*, 2007(1).

6. See Qin Yaqing, "The National Identity, Strategic Culture and Security Interests—Three Assumptions of the Relations between China and the International Community," *World Economics and Politics*, 2003(1).

INDEX

ABOUT THE AUTHOR

Jin Canrong is professor, associate dean, and PhD advisor in diplomacy of the School of International Studies at Renmin University of China. He also serves as dean of the Academic Committee of the Center for International Energy Strategy Studies at Renmin University of China, deputy director of the Center for American Studies at Renmin University of China, vice president of the China National Association of International Studies, and distinguished research fellow of the Research Bureau of the National People's Congress of China.

CPSIA information can be obtained at www.ICGtesting.com
Printed in the USA
BVOW02s2138180115

383712BV00007B/33/P